RESTAURANT & BAR
MARKETING II

HACKING HUMAN NATURE

ERIK SHELLENBERGER

RESTAURANT & BAR MARKETING II: HACKING HUMAN NATURE

Copyright © 2019 by Erik Shellenberger

All rights reserved. This book or any portion thereof may not be reproduced or used in any manner whatsoever without the express written permission of the publisher except for the use of brief quotations in a book review.

Cover Photography: Daveed Benito

Cover Photo Location: Second Story Liquor Bar, Scottsdale AZ

Graphic Design: Erik Shellenberger

Audiobook Narration: Erik Shellenberger

Concept and Author: Erik Shellenberger

Publishing services provided by

ISBN-13: 978-1-69538-275-6

Dedicated to my best friend and girlfriend, Amy Quint. Thank you for sticking with me during the long nights working in front of the computer. It was all worth it.

Thank you to my parents for understanding my crazy thought process and always having my back. I love all of you.

CONTENTS

INTRODUCTION 1

SOCIAL MEDIA 3

GOOGLE 17

THE POWER OF SEO 25

THINK LIKE A CONSUMER, NOT A BUSINESS OWNER 37

PRESENTATION IS EVERYTHING 43

THE MINDSET OF THE 1-STAR YELPER 51

THE "IT" FACTOR 59

MENU SCIENCE 65

THE PROCESS OF MAKING THE DINING DECISION 67

WHAT IF? A COMPLETELY NEW RESTAURANT MODEL WAS CREATED 73

THE STORY OF FIREBALL WHISKY 79

MARKETING THE LIVE MUSIC EXPERIENCE 83

LAST CALL 91

LET'S WORK TOGETHER! 95

A SELFISH REQUEST 97

ABOUT THE AUTHOR 99

INTRODUCTION

I'm sitting here writing this book on New Year's Eve 2018/2019. To some people it may seem ironic that a guy who calls himself a bar expert is home working on New Year's Eve, the "Super Bowl" of nightlife. Chances are you're also in the business and you wholeheartedly understand. I steer clear of "amateur nights" and other red-letter holidays that bring out the worst traits human nature reveals once you add alcohol. The drama. The complainers. The criers and the fighters. The 1-star Yelpers.

I have realized that I've become a bit obsessed with figuring out how to illustrate and clearly explain what brings customers into a certain restaurant and not the identical one across the street. This book contains my thoughts, both opinions and hard data alike. This information has a very short shelf life because of how fast technology moves; there are constants, however, that will live on as long as humans exist.

The status quo of today's restaurant and bar marketing field is just plain screwed. Most places employ the server or bartender who needs more hours as their "Marketing Director." They put the uneducated and unresearched people in charge of driving traffic to their business. Successfully bringing customers in the door is based on strategy and data, not the tool that happens to be the most fun, the one that anyone can operate, like social media.

You wouldn't hire a person with zero cooking experience as your head chef. You wouldn't hire a person with no management experience as your GM. But now more than ever, people with absolutely zero marketing experience are being assigned the Marketing Director position. Hell, I used to be one of them.

"Nurse Alexis, you've been our nurse for a year now. We've been watching you closely, and we think you're ready to tackle open-heart surgery. We understand you've never done one before but you can learn as you go. A few people may end up flatlining, but what the hell, we'll chalk that up to a lesson learned. Now grab that scalpel and start cutting. Good luck. If you need help we'll be downstairs in the cafeteria."

If this is how you treat your business, your livelihood, your children's inheritance, then you can also expect it to die a slow, painful death.

SOCIAL MEDIA

Marketing a bar or restaurant is now synonymous with the term "social media." Social media is fun. Social media is entertaining. It is visual. Your staff is very likely active on social media every day. But here in 2019 social media is less and less effective, to the point of being worthless, thanks to the recent algorithm changes with Facebook and Instagram. Remember this—social media is only a channel through which to transmit your ideas. This is a common-sense notion that is surprisingly forgotten these days. When a "plan" is rarely developed in the first place, and then a half-assed attempt is pumped through a channel that hardly anyone will see, things tend to break down.

Social media, for the most part, is not measurable. Restaurants and bars routinely measure success through data and numbers. Good owners and managers can tell you every metric from food cost to pour costs to bottom-line profit percentages. Rarely if ever can they measure marketing success through social media. Management has no clue as to its success or failure. And somehow, this is accepted. Social media gets a pass for some mysterious reason.

The REAL impact of social media in 2020 and beyond.

> *I have a client who unfortunately had an owner pass away who was the only one who had the social media passwords. For almost exactly an entire year, they were locked out of their social accounts and there was zero activity on them. We recovered their passwords and started posting again a year after losing access. We now had a unique situation and usable data to show the effectiveness and*

> *impact that social had on the bottom line. During the year of zero social activity, the business was actually UP by 10% over the year prior, which used social media! That's not to say that using social hurt them, but in this case it certainly didn't bring anything to the bottom line.*

What's worse is that a marketing approach that the owner, GM, or manager would like to see is rarely the one that will actually be effective. Through no fault of their own. Most bar managers do not have a background in marketing. Most managers, GMs, and the ones calling the shots at the store level did not sign up to be a marketing expert. They are most likely bartenders and servers who worked their way up the ranks to a managerial position. Just like me.

In today's "Instagrammable" environment, we have to evolve and produce an equally Instagrammable product. A visual product will make for a successful marketing plan. Today more than ever, presentation is everything. You can pay someone to show the public pictures of your boring-ass burger, or you can create a visually amazing edible product that the public will want to post on their own social media pages for you. For free!

The best, most successful restaurants and bars are immune to marketing. They don't need it. When word of mouth is all you need to survive and thrive, you win! Success in this business is self-perpetuating. A great customer experience obviously improves word of mouth. Word of mouth is the single most effective avenue for bringing people in the door. And it's free. With enough word of mouth marketing, all other marketing tools become obsolete.

Restaurant and bar marketing is the simple art of figuring out what path a hungry consumer is taking while seeking out a place to eat, and meeting him or her there. Period. My last book, *Restaurant & Bar*

Marketing, mentioned "The Fishbowl vs. the Ocean" concept of where we find customers and where they find us. I will give a brief refresher of this here as well. In today's market, this is of paramount value.

This book is filled with way more marketing tools that do *not* work than ones that do. I do this for one simple reason—to keep your marketing spend to a minimum. The more money you keep in your accounts, the happier I am.

Yes, I own a restaurant and bar marketing company and I do charge clients for my services. But I'm not here to sell you on shit. I'd rather give you every secret I've got, all contained within this book. So before you spend potentially thousands of dollars on some bullshit app that no one will ever download, before you hire a social media team to burn through your marketing budget, before you spend countless man-hours trying to create a product for which there is no market, before you buy another bottle of snake oil, read on.

The Ineffectiveness of Social Media Marketing

Ok, let's get this one out of the way up front. If you've read my last book or have seen anything I've posted anywhere, you know I'm not buying the hype that comes with social media marketing. I enjoy passing on my research and providing value. I have zero qualms with giving away the results of every ounce of research I do for free. There will never be a *"Do you like what you've seen so far? Now click on this special link and give me your 99 bucks, and I'll give out my big secret"* message in my writing or any similar type of horseshit.

When it comes to a restaurant's or bar's social media channels trying to entice customers for a visit, the results are at an all-time low and will continue to drop. Why? Money. Instagram and Facebook are publicly traded companies and have to answer to shareholders. The free-ride days are now well behind us. Combine that with today's sea of awful content and we have a perfect storm of failure. Here is a quick breakdown of what social media's effectiveness will be in 2020:

At the time of this writing, the Facebook and Instagram algorithms have censored our business's posts down to about a maximum of a 10% reach. Meaning only 10% of your followers will ever actually see your posts. When you apply the basic rules of advertising to this, the results are dismal at best. So, for example, if you have 5000 followers between Facebook and Instagram (the only two platforms that matter) 10% of that, or 500 people, will actually see your posts. Now apply the 1% rule of advertising, meaning about 1% of consumers that see your message will actually take action. So we're left with 5. Now ask yourself what you're paying to get these 5 people in the door. Or an easier way to calculate this is to take your total number of followers and hack off 3 digits. Ouch!

Social Media = Tinder for Business

If you think about it, your restaurant's social media profiles are a hell of a lot like a Tinder profile. On both platforms you're trying to "close," right? You're putting out a three-second version of yourself to either be accepted or rejected by the person on the other end. For you old folks, myself included, who aren't familiar with Tinder, it's a dating app. It will show you a picture of a person of the opposite sex (or whatever you're into) and, based on their physical attractiveness alone, you either swipe right if you like what you see or swipe left if not. If the person on the other end also swipes right, it's a match and in theory you live happily ever after and settle down together somewhere in the Cleveland suburbs. Or bang in a dirty nightclub bathroom stall, the results vary. You both get about three seconds or less to make your move. That's the average attention span of humans living in today's online world, both with dating and when deciding if they like your restaurant.

Just like social media, Tinder is simply a channel through which to broadcast yourself.

Remember that. If your social media approach has failed you, it's because your plan, or content, failed. Saying "social media doesn't work" is like saying Tinder doesn't work because every time you try and grab that girl's attention, you open with "Yo, you DTF?" and they go running! Once in a blue moon maybe this works, but not enough to keep the doors open.

"But Erik, aren't you also saying social media doesn't work?" Well, yes. Kinda. I'm saying it's increasingly competitive and expensive. The benefits rarely outweigh the costs. Very few actually succeed. What used to work a decade ago is entirely worthless today. Years ago you could probably "get some action" a lot easier because it was a numbers game. If your profile is seen by tens of thousands of girls, one of them is *sure* to bite. These days, with an all-time-low number of girls seeing your profile, to get anywhere you have to be better, more attractive, and offer an obviously better value than the next guy within our three-second attention span. These days, the restaurant equivalent of the shirt-off-ab-guy-holding-a-puppy-and-kissing-his-grandma all-in-one picture is what it takes to get anywhere.

***"So it's all about looks? Isn't that kind of shallow?"* Yep, it is.**

Whether it's the potential customer on Facebook or the girl on the other end of Tinder who knows *zero* about you, what else is there to go on after knowing you for three seconds? When you start taking your posts seriously and produce a better product, "girls" (customers) will start to take notice. When your social media presence is the equivalent of a Tinder profile using a grainy cell phone pic of you wearing some shitty T-shirt with mustard stains on it, looking like you haven't showered in weeks, do you really expect to close using that approach?

Clean yourself up. Take a shower. Hit the gym. Be the most aesthetically pleasing metaphorical version of yourself possible. When you think of your business's social media presence in correlation to this "guy" on Tinder, the correct approach will become clearer. Ask yourself—would you date you? Would you visit your restaurant based on your social media posts alone?

Remember, the other half of the "decline of social media" equation comes from Facebook and Instagram having to turn a handsome profit, and to keep those profits increasing year after year. You may be the single most handsome some-bitch on Tinder, but if your profile is seen by only a few girls, the results will be meager and short-lived. Sure, it may be a great first drunken weekend on the futon but what about the next week? And the week after that?

That's when you have to start paying for it. You now have to pay both Facebook and Instagram for additional eyeballs on your profile. And keep paying. Week after week. Year after year. Very soon the laws of diminishing returns will kick in and the costs will outweigh the return. Now you're buying a metaphorical dinner for girls who go to "powder their nose real quick" never to be seen from again.

Total Facebook Interactions

- Q1 2017: 29,105,737,101
- Q2 2017: 22,958,328,653
- Q3 2017: 22,924,282,614
- Q4 2017: 20,170,067,666
- Q1 2018: 15,951,949,262
- Q2 2018: 12,819,892,655

Source: Buffer

There is an exception to "paying for it." If you host live music and book headlining acts, by all means throw some money at these shows and get some great exposure. If your brother's deadbeat roommate is playing acoustic guitar on Tuesdays for a beer tab, paying Instagram for more reach would never pay off, however. Another great place to put your money when it comes to social media is with experts who know what they're doing. A good marketing guy who does this for a living is data based, not opinion based. These guys set up systems that can track consumer behavior through online funnels and sales channels that are almost 100% measurable, the polar opposite of your hostess posting shitty iPhone pictures on Mondays, Wednesdays, and Fridays with terrible lighting.

If you were forced to walk down a dark, unknown alley in some sketchy-ass foreign country all by yourself and asked to just "figure it out," it would feel a bit scary. Would you rather have a guide with you who knows the area, the local customs, and how to talk his way out of anything? Or does "winging it" sound appealing?

There are countless business books out there that go into an insane amount of depth concerning social media tips and tricks. I'm not that guy. All that 1% of the 1% of your potential audience bullshit is just that. Don't focus on a certain hashtag technique or the "perfect post description" nonsense I hear a lot. When it comes to your online presence and social media approach, one thing ALWAYS works. **Be attractive.** Like Tinder, if the hungry customer on the other end of the phone is scrolling past your restaurant for three seconds or less, would they stop in based on your posts?

For your average-looking burger joint with stark white walls and little detail or interest, a cafeteria-looking dining room, and a staff who looks like they rolled out of bed an hour ago and it's 2:00pm, failure is a pretty sure bet. Now imagine putting that look on social media. Often, places do more harm than good this way. I've been to places and had a decent meal and *then* checked out their Instagram page only to see burgers that look like warmed over three-day-old dog food in between what looks like a yellow-ish hockey puck for a bun. Had I seen that prior to coming in the door, I wouldn't have.

#IHateHashtags!

I'll spare you another long #hashtag rant and keep it simple.

Hashtags have their place in the world but bars and restaurants are not it. If you have a national brand or a product that is shippable anywhere in the country or world, then hashtags are awesome. If you have restaurant locations in every small town or big city in the country, like McDonald's, then hell yes, hashtag away! If you have one or a few locations, a "global search term," which is what a hashtag is, is absolutely worthless for bringing people in the door.

Furthermore, these days the overuse or misuse of hashtags could get your post flagged as spam and *no one* will ever see it. Hashtags may bring more impressive-looking impression numbers and will sometimes "look" like they are successful, but let me ask you this. If you use *#foodie* and some wannabe food critic in Brooklyn sees your post for a restaurant that's located in Omaha, Nebraska, is this really going to convert into business for said restaurant? Not a chance in hell!

Post Insights

Actions taken from this post

Profile Visits — 9

Discovery ⓘ

689

Accounts reached
17% weren't following you

Follows	0
Reach	689
Impressions	887
From Home	712
From Profile	126
From Hashtags	4
From Other	45

Go to the "insights" section of your own Instagram page and check out how many people *actually* found your post from a hashtag; it's all measurable. Is it worth potentially getting flagged as spam to get your post in front of another four people? Most likely from some other corner of the planet?

I will also repeat that I'm probably the only person that will ever tell you this. Everyone else who is a "social media expert" will wholeheartedly and adamantly disagree with me. They looooooove hashtags. After all, the increased numbers make them look like their posts are successful. If likes and impressions actually equaled money, then cute kittens would be the biggest ballers on the planet.

The most hilariously insane misuse of hashtags is when a business hashtags themselves. Meaning they use #eriksbarandgrill or whatever in every post. What the fuck is this supposed to do, anyway? It's like leaving your phone number on your voicemail message. It's like leaving a link to your website on your website. It's like introducing yourself to your best friend. Redundancy at its most ridiculous! This is a classic example of doing what the guy next to you is doing without a clue as to why he's doing it. For some reason, shit like this spreads like chlamydia at Coachella.

> *Picture a huge room full of people all taking a test that no one studied for. Everyone starts copying the answers from the person next to them. Now we have a huge group of people with different versions of the wrong answer. They all assume the person next to them has it all figured out so they will simply steal their answers and move on. This is the nature of today's social media marketing.*

Chances are, your successful neighbor down the street doesn't know what they're doing any more than you do, they just have some factor that drives business that you may be lacking. They may have a better location. They may have the best burger in four counties. They may have just gotten lucky.

I want to get the whole social media subject out of the way up front because I don't want to go any further down this rabbit hole. I want to knock it out early on so we can move on to what really works. When talking to restaurant and bar people about marketing, they use the words "social media" interchangeably with "marketing." Social is only a very small slice of a very big pie. So let's get on with the rest of the pie.

Hire Accordingly

The right professional or, depending on the size of your operation, team of professionals, can make or break you. Restaurants of the past have definitely gotten away without professional marketing people. Some are in the perfect location and rely 100% on foot traffic. Some have the best damn ribs around. Some are owned by the nicest people you've ever met and you can't help but stop in just to talk to them. Some just got lucky.

Unless you fall into one of these categories, you need to market. And market correctly. The knowledge in this book will teach you what the experts know. Once educated, you could possibly do most of it yourself. Chances are you are more passionate about your business than anyone else in your employ. Chances are you may "know how it's done" but don't have the kind of time to pull it off correctly. So make that determination early on. If a professional is needed, go with that and stick with it.

The Tourist Market

Just like building a house, you use the right tool for the job. If you're in a tourist economy and rely almost exclusively on tourist business, social media is worthless. Here is a question I ask my potential clients in this situation all the time.

How can someone follow you on social media who hasn't ever heard of you?

I can tell most of the time this never crossed their minds in the least. These owners certainly aren't dumb. They've just never thought about it on those terms. Marketing on Facebook and Instagram is such a knee-jerk reaction, it's rarely thought through in practical terms. Again, unless you have a tiki bar on the beach of a popular Americanized beach club somewhere in Jamaica, like young Flannigan did in the movie *Cocktail*, you need to advertise using the correct tools. Social media is for locals. It's for people who have heard of you. It's for cultivating a one-time customer into a regular. It's for brand awareness. It's to keep your regulars informed of upcoming events like headlining live music shows. It's NOT for people who haven't heard of you.

Can you imagine who would have followed the Facebook page of that little beach tiki bar in the movie? What the hell would be the point of even having one? Even if *Cocktail* wasn't made pre-social media, Flannigan surely would have read about this in one of those self-help books he kept under the bar. Flannigan relies on 100% walk-up foot traffic from tourists that the resort brings in. If you aren't in this fortunate situation but are still in a tourist market, then what? Your favorite tools should be Google, Yelp, and TripAdvisor. For some reason, these are common-sense tools for the tourist but are rarely optimized by the restaurant marketing to these same tourists.

If you are in the weird grey area of being in a tourist market yet you're located a half a block away from the action, these three tools *will* make or break you. Unless you also have a huge local cult following, which rarely happens. You need to have a bigger, better presence here than your competition. I grew up in tourist cities and there is an unspoken rule of thumb that exists in almost every one of them. Bars and restaurants either have a tourist customer base *or* they are for locals. Rarely do the two meet. If you live in Vegas, you will steer clear of the strip at all costs. I did when I lived there. Now that I don't live there anymore, I visit the Las Vegas strip every time I'm in town.

What if I told you…

…that there was a social media platform out there that, if used correctly, could bring 50,000—sometimes 100,000 impressions—to your brand in a single month? Then what if I said that you can either post to this platform or not, it doesn't matter much.

Then what if I told you that this platform is made up of consumers looking to make a buying decision *right then*? With traditional social media, restaurants tend to be seen as annoyances when we inject a picture of our cheeseburger into the user's feed when they're just trying to enjoy puppy and kitten videos. However, on this platform, *they* are actively seeking *us* out.

On this platform, people don't have to "follow" or "like" you to see your brand, it's open to everyone, and *all* businesses are here. This captive audience doesn't require discounts or coupons to walk in the door. They are all willing and able to pay full price. The best part is, traffic on this platform is totally measurable. Not only "impressions" like traditional social media, but *you can measure the number of people who get directions to your restaurant and walk in the door to spend money!*

What have I just described?

GOOGLE

The Worst Game of "Telephone" Ever

In my last book, I glossed over the SEO (search engine optimization) process because it's so mind-numbingly nerdy and technical that most of you would definitely find better things to do than read that chapter. Well here's an analogy that I think paints the picture in an easy-to-understand way. Remember the game "Telephone" we played as school kids where we would get in a circle and try to successfully convey a message accurately from one kid to the next? The first person whispers a phrase into the ear of the kid next to them, and they whisper it to the next kid in the circle and so on. The phrase would get more and more jacked up as it went on. When it got back to the beginning, the last kid would have to say the phrase out loud and it was undoubtedly something completely different. Often it was something so far removed from the original message that it had become a whole new concept altogether.

This Is How the Internet Treats Your Brand

As well as every other website that online directories try to index and identify. Think of search engines like Google, Bing, and Yahoo, as well as social media sites, as "directories," another name for a "list of websites." Except there are hundreds or thousands of directories out there with which your online presence may come in contact. They all share information with each other at light speed. And they suck at it. It's the quickest, shittiest game of telephone ever. Have you ever discovered your hours are incorrect online somewhere? Or a customer gets pissed because they can't order the Spaghetti and Meatballs, which you removed from the menu years ago? Here's the kicker—the more inconsistencies and wrong information your business lists, the worse Google will rank you in a simple search like "Restaurants near me."

Unless you get a handle on your online presence, these directories are like the Wild West. Wrong info can spread like wildfire. You may have inaccurate info on some oddball directory like 411.com (the internet's version of calling information back in the day). Well, who cares if it's wrong on there, right? Who's really going to find your business there anyway? Google will. Google sees and knows all of this. When your missing and inconsistent info is spread all over the place via this terrible, invisible game of telephone, your business will suffer because your Google ranking will suffer. Google looks at it like this—if you don't care about your ranking, why should they?

For bars and restaurants who fit this model of being in a hard-to-find location yet based in a tourist market, optimizing your Google presence is of paramount importance. I have a client who has a restaurant called the Elbow Room which is 100 yards off of the Hollywood Walk of Fame in Los Angeles. A perfect scenario for this example. He has a great operation, awesome food, friendly people, and cheap drinks for the area. All of the ingredients for success are there. Except the customers.

I started to optimize his bar's presence in Google. I made sure he showed up in a Google search *above* his competition. Within about 90 days, he was showing up in the Holy Grail of online real estate—the map (or pin marker) section of a Google search, from which he was previously missing. His inconsistent contact info was now correct. His brand was added to hundreds of new directories. His brand was ranking higher and higher by the week. Before we started,

679 people saw his bar in a Google search in a 30-day period. Exactly four months later, he had rocketed up to 18,195 eyeballs on his brand in a single month!!

That's great and all, but how does that equate to people walking in the door?

Well, I'm glad you asked that. You know the little button on your phone when you're doing a Google search that says "get directions"? This metric makes SEO 100% measurable right down to someone walking in your door to spend money. Let's see social media do that!

> *What this metric measures is the number of random people finding a new business in a Google search, liking what they see, and getting directions to make a visit. What I refer to as a "Right here, right now" search. These people are obviously unfamiliar with this business since they need directions. They are most likely tourists in this case. They were unaware that this business had existed until this search.* ***There is a very good chance that they do not follow this business on social media. Again, you can't "like" a business if you don't know it exists.***

This client went from 99 people who hit the "get directions" button per month to 628 in just a three-month period! What is it worth to you to increase new business by 534%? It's a lot cheaper than you may think. To put all of this into perspective, my services for this client cost him the equivalent of raising the "get directions" metric by 8. We raised it by 529! Marketing that is measurable right down to the guy walking in the door leaves zero room for speculation or opinion. That is why my business Bar Marketing Basics is based off of this concept. Social media can't make these claims. Not even close.

Of course some of this increase is organic and not because of my efforts. Some may be seasonal changes. Some may be Uber drivers, although the *proportion* of Uber drivers using the "get directions" button wouldn't change with SEO work. Once these variables are removed, SEO still remains the single most impactful, measurable way to increase business for a bar or restaurant in this situation. My numbers are all taken from Google analytics directly and not from my sources. I couldn't manipulate these numbers if I wanted to. This is what something like this looks like on paper.

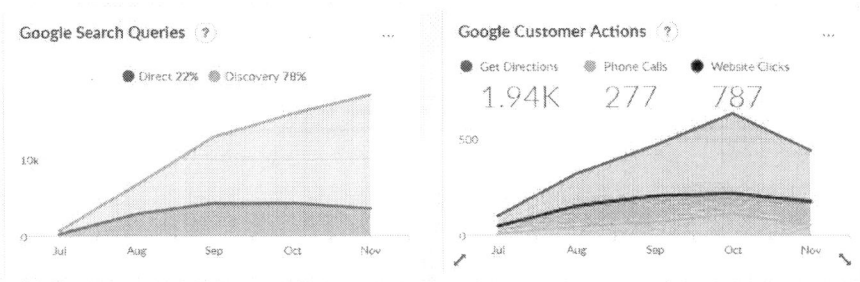

"Direct" traffic is the measurement of people looking specifically for this client, not an open-ended search. Since we already have this guy, I'm not concerned with direct traffic. "Discovery" is the people who found this client through an open-ended Google keyword search like "restaurants near me."

So you say you don't need SEO because, if you Google yourself, you show up in that search, right? I talked to a prospective client who told me exactly this. I said if you Google the name of your own business (direct traffic), you'd *better* show up! With a broad search like "Restaurants in Phoenix" he was nowhere to be found, even though he was sitting in his restaurant at the time of the search. We all know the drill—if you do a search like this, your business will probably show up. But how far do you have to zoom in on your location until your place pops up? If you have to zoom all the way in until it finally shows up, you are at a pretty big disadvantage if your customers also find you (or don't find you) this way.

SEO can put your brand in front of more eyeballs. It cannot force people into your business.

Your brand is still only as good as your three-second aesthetic here as well. Human nature usually goes a little something like this: People will start with a Google search. Once they find your business, they will check out a few pictures, reviews, etc. and often go to your Instagram or Facebook page to see more of what your place is about. Based on that they will make their decision to either stop in or keep scrolling. When your Google presence is optimized, you *will* show up as an option more often, there is no question about that part. If your brand is unappealing or doesn't live up to the expectation of the consumer, they *will not* pay you a visit, no matter how good your SEO guy is!

RESTAURANT & BAR MARKETING II

GETTING FOUND ONLINE FROM THE CUSTOMER'S PERSPECTIVE

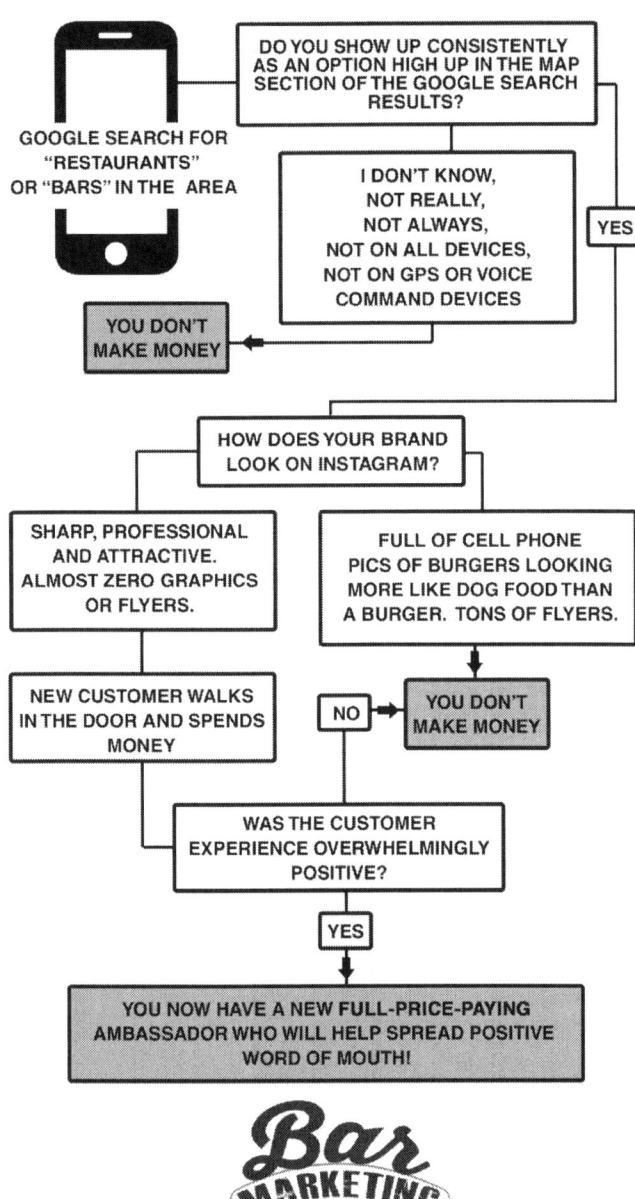

Remember, Google customers are all *full-price-paying* customers. They do not require a discount to walk in the door, unlike most social media calls-to-action.

Play to Your Audience

When I use the Tinder reference and say to "be attractive," I mean to be attractive to the audience you're trying to attract. If you own a dive bar, you don't have to give the illusion that you are a fine-dining joint. People looking for a dive bar don't necessarily need to see the best presentations, the cleanest bar, the highest end liquors. Be the best version of what a dive bar customer is looking for.

There is a dive in Las Vegas right off the strip called the Double Down Saloon that is a favorite of mine. They have a huge sign behind the bar with their long-running drink special of "Ass Juice." They take it one step further and offer the "deal" of "$4 for 1, or 2 for $9" which is obviously not much of a deal at all.

The place is outdated, tacky as hell, dirty, stinky, and just plain gross. It looks like it was abandoned by the owners years ago but for some reason, people kept showing up—my type of place! They have perfected the art of attracting the exact clientele they are going after. The place is filled with punk rockers and blue-collar folks. Every time I've been there, it's been a great time. I've brought groups of girls who were dressed for the clubs later on in the night and had a better time at the Double Down than at the clubs! All for a fraction of the price, of course.

The Double Down is immune to Yelp reviews. They don't care about reviews and honestly don't need them. Their clientele wouldn't ever find a place like this through Yelp anyway. If the Double Down cleaned itself up and started taking their aesthetic seriously, they would definitely fail. They play to their audience and they play perfectly.

If you were at this bar and got served a shitty drink, you'd expect it. If you sat in gum that was on the barstool, you'd probably see that coming anyway. If the bartender uses blatant, loud profanity toward the customers, you'd probably laugh. If this happened at any other type of bar or restaurant, it would be a *huge* problem. At places like this, it's almost anticipated.

The Double Down does what they do well, even if that means being the best version of a disgusting place.

THE POWER OF SEO

With a few exceptions, harnessing the power of Google and SEO is no longer optional, it's required if you want to attract customers who have not yet heard of you. Chances are your competition doesn't know this or doesn't take it seriously, so you have an advantage right out of the gate. If you don't even show up as an option in a customer's search for a new place to grab a drink or a bite to eat, you're missing a huge opportunity. If your hat is not even in the ring and you ignore this "step 1" to attracting new customers, you're missing out on a huge percentage of what brings a new customer through your door.

Here is a breakdown of the importance of SEO by market:

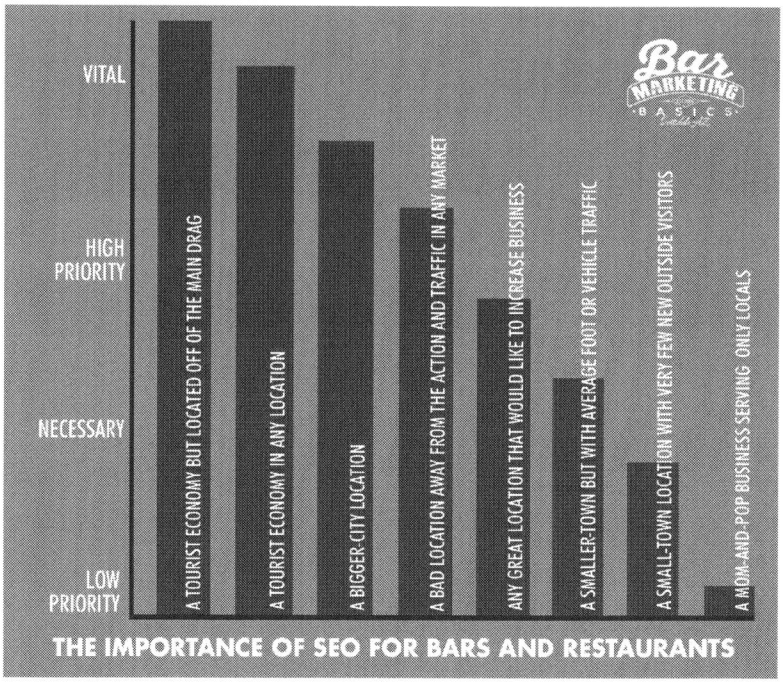

You now know the "why" and "who" of SEO. Search engine optimization is probably the only thing where I will not get into great detail about the "how." It's not that I want to keep some well-guarded trade secret, I just don't want to bore the shit out of my readers! SEO is very boring, monotonous, not visual, un-sexy, and massively complicated. It can also be discouraging because it usually takes 90 days or more until results are even noticed. Because of this, most restaurants don't ever do anything about it. It's not something you can hand over to your hostess to take care of. Most people can't wrap their head around the process, so they choose to ignore it. This is very much to your advantage.

Consistent, Thorough, and Everywhere

I'll provide the basics of SEO without hopefully losing too many of you. Consistency and thoroughness is the backbone of SEO. If you have an online profile, let's say Google or Yelp, and there are 40 different fields to fill out yet you only fill out the bare essentials until the "*ok*" button isn't greyed out anymore so you can move on, this will kill your ranking with Google. Fill out every online profile as accurately and completely as possible. If there is a place to upload 20 pictures of your business, fight the urge to upload your logo and move on because you never did get that photo shoot done. Be prepared and have your assets all on your computer. Upload ALL 20 photos. Google is a lot like your elementary school teacher—it rewards doing a good job and docks you if you're half-assing something.

Keep your name consistent no matter where you are or how many locations you have. EVERY online profile should be uploaded with the exact same info. Meaning if you're in Scottsdale, AZ, don't add "Scottsdale" to the end of your Facebook title. If your place is called "Erik's Bar & Grill" then every title field should read exactly that, and only that. Even if you have ten locations, each one should be titled exactly "Erik's Bar & Grill." Google will use the address field to differentiate the different locations. "Erik's Bar & Grill – Scottsdale" is a rookie mistake.

Backlinks Are (still) King

Backlinks are other websites or directories that have a link back to your website. Technically, your Facebook page, your Yelp profile, Bing, Yahoo, and others like them are all backlinks. These all have that field for you to enter your website, hence creating a link back to your website. The more the better, as long as they are relevant to your business and not some random list of spammy crap that's unassociated with restaurants or bars.

Do not, I repeat, *do not* buy backlinks or try and cheat the system. Google employs the smartest motherfuckers in the world. They'll catch you if you try to take a shortcut. If caught, this will kill your Google ranking and you'll be sent to the doghouse. If you're in a tourist economy, this could kill your business quickly.

So that's kind of it. To start ranking well in Google:

Be consistent.

Be thorough.

Be everywhere.

The surprising part to most people in the restaurant and bar business is that ranking high in Google can be very affordable if the right professional is found. Buying SEO services is like buying a used car. It's worth whatever someone is willing to spend. Its effectiveness is also all over the board. The worst are the overseas telemarketers and robo-callers selling SEO services. Damn, I hate these people! It makes the entire subject repulsive, cheap, and loathsome. It probably goes without saying, but these guys are ineffective clowns with a horrible, spammy marketing approach. If this is how they market *their own* company, how do you think they'll market yours?

When I bring up the subject of SEO to prospective clients, they give me this look like *"You're one of them?"* Definitely not, but sometimes I feel like I'm like the one honest guy handing out coupons for "massages" on the Vegas strip. *"Seriously, it's just a massage and it's actually only $19 total"!* That's what a sleazy-feeling business SEO has become.

It shouldn't cost more than $500/mo. to start ranking well. Usually way less. My services start around half that. The results of SEO should be totally measurable like I mentioned earlier. If your SEO guy is unable to provide accurate, measurable data based on Google analytics, that's a red flag. If they require a contract, that's a red flag as well. If they are able to produce measurable results every month, why would they need a contract?

If you think that's expensive, ask yourself how much you are spending on social media, which you can't measure at all and is totally unproven. Whether it's your money or your time, chances are you are upside down.

Also, when I mention SEO and Google as great tools to leverage, I don't mean Google AdWords (now called Google Ads). The only instance that paying for Google ads pays off in this industry is if you have something specific to mention and promote. Placing a generic ad that basically says *"There are a million options in this area to grab a bite to eat, I'm another one of them. Come eat here"* works out exactly the way you'd expect. A huge waste of money.

If you are a live music venue or have a big one-off event coming up, Google Ads may work for you. It hinges, of course, on how big the event or artist is. Happy Hour doesn't count! Something significant may drive some traffic. Keep in mind these ads show up in the "sponsored" area toward the top of the Google search results, much like the completely worthless "sponsored" area at the top of a Yelp search. Human nature tells our brains to ignore that section altogether and start looking at the first organic result. What makes sponsored areas worse is that, since they appear at the top of quite a lot of the searches performed by the public, the impression numbers look huge. And expensive. They "appear" quite a few times, for which you are paying. They almost never receive any attention. Sponsored ad placement is the online equivalent of the guy on the Vegas strip handing out the *"beautiful girls sent directly to your room"* cards. They are on every corner, all selling the exact same thing, all of which get ignored by 99.9% of the people walking by. You try your hardest to not make eye contact but they still shove these cards in your face every chance they get. Real-life human-sponsored ads.

The sponsored ad section is best reserved for New Year's Eve or other similar red-letter days. Your money is always better spent on organic, long-term SEO.

Keywords and Categories

Just because your restaurant ranks number one for the search term *"Best barbecue restaurants south of Main Street with a brick building"* doesn't mean anyone else is searching for that. You can easily dominate a worthless word. This is one of the biggest mistakes I see with the armchair SEO expert. The big question is, how many *other* people are searching for the same word? The traffic for "BBQ Restaurants" has a totally different search volume than "Barbecue

Restaurants" and "Bar-B-Que Restaurants." These different spellings make all the difference in the world. In this graphic below, you can see that "Scottsdale Restaurants" gets 33,100 searches per month while "Restaurants in Scottsdale" only gets 6600 searches. Even though Google sees them as similar phrases, you can see that subtle changes in wording produce massively different results.

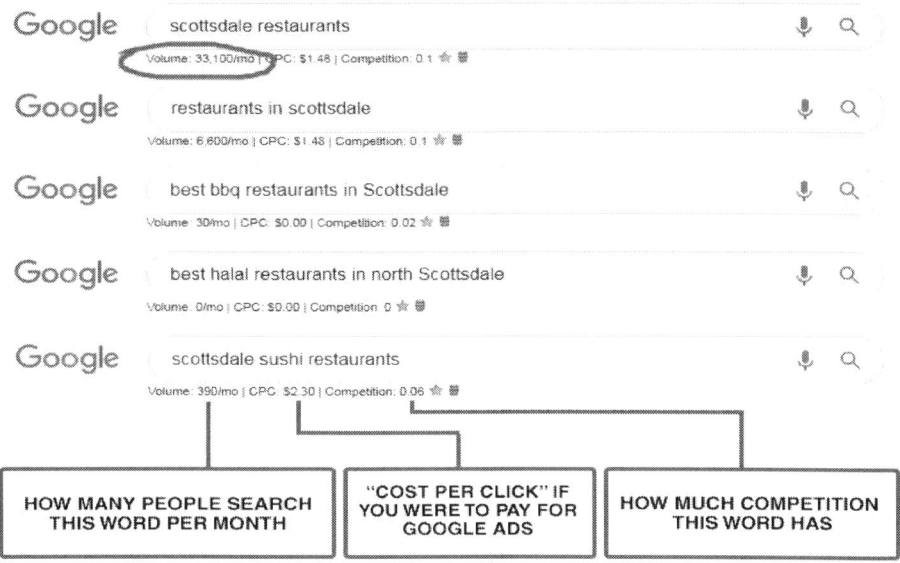

Since you probably just grabbed your computer, typed your favorite key phrase into Google, and didn't see these numbers, I'll let you in on a little trick. *"Keywords Everywhere"* is a Google Chrome extension I use to produce these numbers. So go to your Chrome browser extensions and add this one. Start using an informed approach to optimizing the right words, not just the ones you are guessing. Proper keyword research is considerably more complicated than this but this is a huge step forward compared to pulling random words out of thin air.

You'll definitely want to rank at the top of the high-volume words but always pay attention to "competition." If there is too much competition (0.1 is actually a lot) then going for more niche words or categories may be a better bet. I may be getting a bit deep into the nerd realm here, so please reach out to me if you'd like to learn more at erik@barmarketingbasics.com.

Your Google Categories

Depending on what year it is and who you talk to, there is a difference of opinion when discussing how to categorize your main Google My Business category vs. your subcategories. I categorize all of my restaurant clients' main category as just "Restaurant." Not "Pizza Restaurant" or "Mexican Restaurant," as those are best reserved for the subcategories. I like to cast the widest net possible and no restaurant-based keyword has more reach than plain ol' "Restaurant."

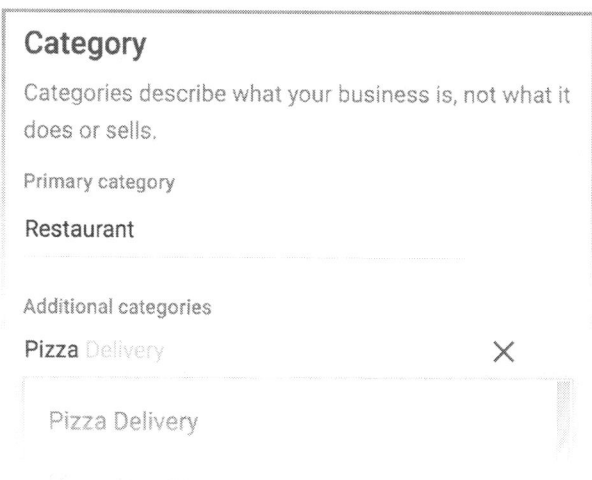

(Access this info by going to google.com/business)

I don't have to go into the stats when it comes to just how many of us use Google on a daily basis, so I'll spare you those. Let's just say everyone has a computer in their pocket and one of the biggest *"Right here, right now"* searches involves where to eat or drink. Statistically, Google brings in way more money to the bottom line than social media ever will now and especially in 2020 and beyond. By doing the simple basics and optimizing your Google My Business (GMB) page, you will have a huge advantage over your competition, who probably doesn't pay attention to anything resembling SEO. This is the good news. The bar is set extremely low so even the simplest of efforts within your Google My Business account will produce results. For free.

This is the part that I could never understand. Restaurants use social media because they understand how to use it (or at least their staff does). They use visual ads and tangible marketing assets. Rarely, if ever, do they optimize their Google presence. When I ask restaurant owners why they haven't taken this step, they always reply with something like "I don't have any idea how to do that." They recognize the importance but rarely are steps taken to improve this area. No one is expecting the average restaurant owner to be able to tackle SEO. I don't know how to repair today's computer-driven cars, but when my car breaks down, I don't throw it away because I don't happen to know how to fix it! When it comes to improving your Google search engine ranking, hiring a professional is vital.

Search Smart

As I mentioned, just because you Google the name of your business or even "restaurants near me" and you show up doesn't mean your potential customer will get the same results. All devices use different mapping software and there are several other factors that will greatly skew these results. Whether or not your device's GPS is on will also make a big difference in ranking.

You know all those times you sat at your favorite table in the back of your own restaurant and Googled your own business? Remember how great your restaurant ranked? You were at the top of the search results for damn near everything! You've dominated the Google search engine results! Before you pat yourself on the back for ranking so well by doing, well, nothing, keep in mind that the businesses in the closest proximity at the time of your search will always show up first. Unfortunately, your prospective customers will not exactly see the same results. Their search engine results will be significantly different for searching the *same exact word*.

Google search results differ depending on quite a few factors, including but not limited to:

Device – The iPhone, iMac, PC, and Samsung Galaxy all use different mapping software. I once sat in a restaurant management's corporate office and was being asked why they didn't rank like they'd expected in search engine results. We were in the unique situation of coincidentally having all four of these devices in the same room at the same time. We all Googled the exact same word and, sure enough, we got four completely different results ranging from #1 to nonexistent.

Gmail or Google account – Whether you are logged into your Gmail account or not will also affect search engine results. Your account remembers your past searches and will likely display those first. Chances are, your restaurant will rank *really* well in this case, which in reality is a false result unique to your own computer and account.

GPS – If your GPS (or location services) is turned on, Google will display results in your geographical area first. Without GPS you will most likely have to use a geographical limiter like "Restaurants in Scottsdale" as opposed to just "Restaurants." Next time you try to find your own restaurant in a search like this, do it from across town while logged out of your Gmail account. These results unfortunately will be much, much worse.

Here is the elephant-in-the-room question. *"Yeah, but how do I know your SEO efforts created these results? How do I know this wouldn't have just happened organically?"*

There are two different constants to keep in mind. New businesses will of course start from zero Google exposure and will grow over the months. Your brand-new business's Google visibility will organically grow naturally, no question. Normal growth is 10–20% or so per month, plateauing around the six month point. This is a very broad stat though. Real organic growth varies considerably from concept to concept and so it is really hard to assign a number. The plateau is almost always guaranteed during the first year and growth will be slow from this point, if at all. Good SEO will grow your Google exposure 200, 400, 600% during the first year. Sometimes increases north of 1000% are possible.

Established restaurants or bars that have been around for years are well into the plateau point of their organic Google exposure. Hundreds of percentage points of increase in impressions are ONLY possible with a good SEO approach. I got one of my clients, who has been around for well over a decade, over ten times the amount of impressions we started with over a yearlong SEO campaign. A 1000% increase from an established business!

I've often showed clients this insane amount of traffic, including the increase in *"Get Directions"* numbers. When we discuss an increase to their bottom line, they often agree the increases were in parallel. The crazy part to me is when certain clients of the past have listened a little too closely to a PR person, social media expert, hostess, or other uninformed person out there and eventually canceled. No amount of mathematical proof can convince them that I was costing them WAY less than I was making them. Sometimes emotions are far more powerful than logic. Some of the biggest compliments I can get are when these clients sign back up a few months later. "Ok you win, we did see a significant drop in new customers after we canceled. Let's get this Google thingy going again." Done!

THINK LIKE A CONSUMER, NOT A BUSINESS OWNER

The crap that people pass off as "marketing materials" these days is laughable. I can tell in a second if a certain social media post or promotion followed the direction of a manager or business owner verbatim. If the designer did *exactly* what the owner or GM asked for, it usually looks like complete shit.

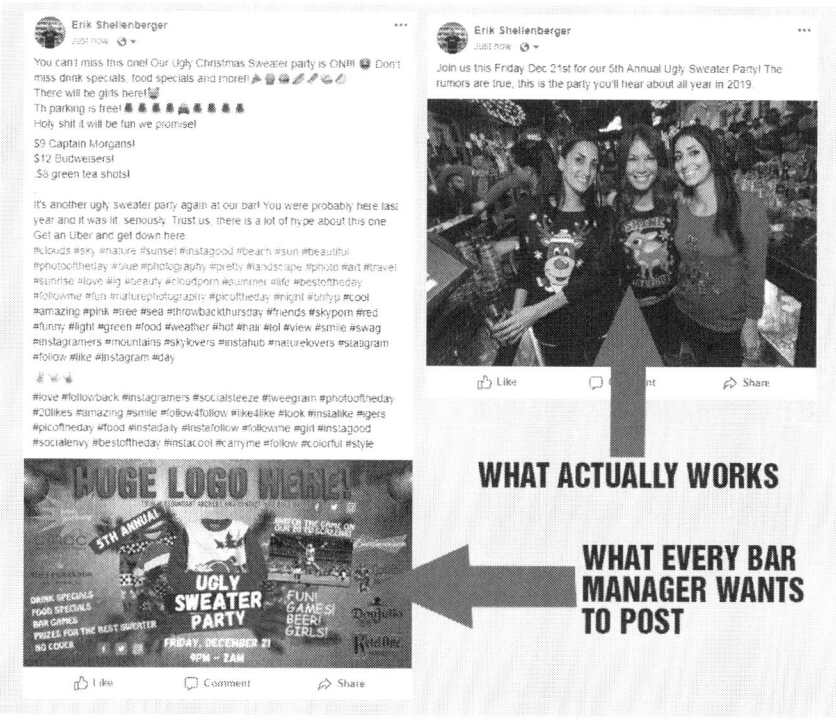

Posts like this colossal clusterfuck on the left are a monumental ode to *"how it's NOT done."* As a consumer, the left post hurts my eyes! Busy-ass flyers like this one not only get censored by Facebook and

Instagram like I mentioned in my last book, but consumers will also ignore these entirely because of the information overload. Human nature hates being advertised to, but it does like being entertained. The minute you start thinking like a consumer is when the entertainment you provide will start making you money.

Remember the three-second rule of holding someone's attention? Keep this in mind when creating graphics. Actually, try to not make graphics at all. Great, relevant photos will always trump flyers. And this is coming from a graphic designer who made a living making flyers for over a decade. The photo on the right of the girls behind the bar will grab way more attention. It's authentic and true to the brand because (let's assume) these are the actual bartenders who work at this bar. You don't need paragraphs and bullet points. This one picture tells the entire story. It's all that is required. And the best part? It's WAY cheaper and easier than getting a flyer made!

Like I mentioned in the intro of this book, "marketing experts" are being replaced by the server or hostess who wants more hours than the restaurant can give them. Since they don't want to lose the employee, they are handed the illustrious position of *"Marketing Director."* Sounds important! I'm no better actually. I most definitely came up like this myself. I was a guy who knew how to make an ok website, that's it. My employer at the time wanted a flyer made so I learned Photoshop, and so on. With no background in marketing and no education in this field, I did what almost everyone does today. We use our own personal opinions. Nowadays, one person's opinion seems to prevail, and most of them are gawd-awful.

Management's and the owners' opinions are equally shitty, usually worse actually. The people calling the shots would like nothing more than a sea of busy flyers in their overly complicated posts. They all look at the world through the lens of *"This is what I would like the world to see."* The question should be turned on its head and what should be asked is, *"As a consumer, what would I like to see?"* When this alternate lens is used and personal opinion is thrown out, you start to connect with the public.

Your opinion doesn't matter. My opinion doesn't matter. The only opinion that matters is public opinion.

Go to YouTube and search "Make my logo bigger cream."

This is a hilarious illustration of this concept. It shows how a professional, educated, and beautiful promotional design can be destroyed by one person's uneducated opinion of what *they* want the world to see. This is every graphic designer's nightmare. To avoid this, the guy who creates the *design* should be a different person from the guy creating the *content*. In most cases, the design guy looks at this from a right-brained, artistic angle. The content guy is in the opposite camp and should focus on facts and accuracy. When the content guy tries to cross over into the design realm is when the majority of these horrible-graphic issues happen.

"Restaurant Marketing Experts" are running critically low on the "Expert" part.

A while ago I made the decision to remove myself from the creative aspect of restaurant and bar marketing and focus exclusively on SEO and Reputation Management, the two things that are more or less void of a creative, visual aspect, as well as opinion. Back when I did a little bit of everything marketing related, I'm positive that after leaving several meetings where I mentioned this above scenario and suggested a clean, simple approach, I was promptly crossed off the list. The mind-blowing part is that most restaurant management groups want to hire a "marketing professional" that will execute exactly what the group would like to see, hence eliminating the "professional" part.

Since I'm the farthest thing from a "yes man," I opted out of the creative aspect altogether. I was done spreading someone else's poorly thought-out version of some other successful company's marketing approach.

PR companies don't like me much. Some PR companies, however, are awesome all around. Others send a sales representative out to talk to the client, or the restaurant owners. Salespeople are inherently not educated in the technical aspects of the business. Not really their fault, it's just not their area of expertise. They speak in terms of flashy-sounding things like "action item list," "paradigm shift," and "a three-pronged approach," which all give me a giant fucking headache. When I'm brought in to "work in collaboration" with the PR firm, it rarely ends well. It actually always ends poorly. I can't listen to PR reps spew nonsense and stats that may have been true decades ago but are worthless in today's market. Any sort of minor correction from me is deemed an attack for some reason, and I'm quickly squeezed out of the equation. Thankfully, I'd rather stick to talking to a client with easy-to-understand terms than try to baffle them with bullshit.

In this scenario I'm not just the sales guy, but I'm also the nerd who does all of the work to make said results happen. I'm the guy who is educated and researched. I wear all of the hats at the same time. I don't work well with theories, I work in the realm of measurable results. I don't have a "team" that all work in collaboration at a snail's pace. I am the entire team, which PR companies seem to hate. I recently had a meeting with an ex-client who wanted to bring my SEO services back. In the 30 years that they had been open, this was the only time they saw the younger demographic they had wanted actually walk through the door, along with record sales numbers. This client was pretty old school and didn't really speak on a technical level, but the bottom-line numbers and new faces didn't lie. The husband in this husband-and-wife team didn't understand what I did and canceled after a little over a year because he could "update their menu online themselves" now that they had a PR company that could update the website. Weird, I didn't even do that for them at any point.

Anyway, after canceling with me and noticing a significant drop in new faces, and of course numbers, the wife asked me to come back in and meet with their PR person in hopes of bringing my SEO services back. Oh boy, here we go again. Her approach was so far removed from the reality of how SEO works that she said on multiple occasions, *"Yeah, we do exactly the opposite of that."* When I tried to correct her on a couple fundamentals of day-one-SEO stuff, she tuned out and started furiously typing away on her computer and refused to look me in the eye for the remainder of the meeting. It was the subtle virtual-middle-finger approach.

Like I said, PR companies don't like me and I have no problem with that. What bugged me is that she was undoubtedly charging this poor couple thousands of dollars per month for a smokescreen of absolute bullshit. I really liked this ex-client of mine and am still a customer of their restaurant to this day. I don't like seeing good people getting fleeced but I wasn't about to get into a war of "who knows their technical nerd-speak better." I think the major issue with PR's hatred of my approach is that SEO is measurable down to the dollar. I can prove with Google Analytics that I make my clients more than I cost them. With PR, this isn't at all possible. We're all left to guess whether or not their approach is working.

In my opinion, PR companies are only successful during the grand-opening phase. If you're thinking you may hire a PR company, please get different opinions from different agencies and ask the tough questions. Ask for proof of results. Not in the form of impressions, in the form of dollars in the door. Post their claims or processes in restaurant and bar owner groups on Facebook. The people in those groups are usually well researched and have some pretty refined bullshit detectors. Don't take anything at face value. Some PR companies are awesome at what they do but like quite a few marketing "professionals" these days, there are more and more bad apples every day giving us all a bad name.

PRESENTATION IS EVERYTHING

Remember the Tinder analogy as it applies to social media? The more attractive you are in three seconds, the better your results will be. If a Tinder profile was applied to the actual product when it comes to bars and restaurants, Barton G in Los Angeles would be part supermodel, part Instagram model, and part porn star. Once you get your customer through the door, presentation is absolutely everything!

When researching restaurants in Los Angeles, we came across Barton G. They had average Yelp reviews. These reviews mentioned average food (some were below average). They mentioned long wait times. Nothing special on the surface. But the presentations—holy shit! They have the most insane, over-the-top presentations I've ever seen, and I've seen quite a lot. Here is the raw power of a solid, unique presentation. We made a reservation, which was *tough* to get in the first place. Even though we made the reservation quite a ways out, prime times were taken so we had to settle for our third-choice time slot.

We showed up and the place was *packed!* The waiting area was totally full, and people were waiting outside and everywhere else they could fit. They were at full capacity, and I'm sure they had to turn people away because there were no more tables available. We got seated and the service was quick and friendly. The atmosphere was dark and sexy. We placed our order and split an entree because we weren't all that hungry and the portions were pretty big. Our server politely told us they had a policy that everyone has to order their own entree, or we could also order an appetizer, which we did.

Our drinks showed up and, damn! The Buddhalicious was served in a martini glass on a wooden plank bridge that took two hands to carry, complete with a foot-tall Buddha statue standing on a bridge with a gong behind him. The drink had dry-ice smoke coming out of it and came complete with a vodka popsicle resting inside it. The other drink was the Enter the Dragon, which was served in an equally impressive platform with a black dragon head background complete with a two-foot-tall banner bearing huge Japanese characters. Dry ice made an appearance in this cocktail as well.

This was just the beginning. We ordered the Lobster Pop-Tarts as the appetizer. We expected, well, Pop-Tarts. When they came, they were huge squares served in an actual full-sized toaster! But not just any toaster. This was one of those cool retro toasters with crazy colors and curved, organic shapes. They use the term "Pop-Tarts" loosely. They were some of the best-looking and best-tasting appetizers I've ever had.

The main courses had to up-the-ante from that point and delivered. The filet mignon came with an actual four-foot-tall metal fork sticking out of it! No exaggeration, this fork was every bit of four feet tall. Looking round the dining room, we saw a salmon dish with a three-foot-tall fishing lure standing up in the back of the dish, which was served on a giant cutting board. They served a "Coastline Crab and Lobster Salad" over a transparent glass container with actual live hermit crabs running around in a separate sealed section just beneath the salad! The whole thing was, of course, also bathed in dry ice for that mysterious effect.

Every single dish we saw came with an over-the-top presentation. We were half eating our meal and half busy checking out everyone else's orders. We saw the Lawn Moo-er, which is a steak served on an actual lawn mower. A fucking full-sized lawn mower! The list goes on. There are dozens of these and they are all unique and very creative.

We had one drink each, we shared an app and shared an entree. Our bill came to over $200 for the two of us. Expensive but worth the experience. The next time we're in LA, we will make it a point to go back to Barton G!

So here is proof that a great presentation can outweigh:

- An average Yelp rating
- Average food reviews
- An exorbitant price tag
- A long wait for a table
- Strict house rules on ordering
- Difficulty getting a reservation

Despite all of this, it was one of the most memorable dining experiences I've ever had. This experience is also now in a book based on restaurant marketing (possibly not the first time). If you talk about Barton G with anyone who's been there, there is always a great story associated with it. The place is legendary.

Here is the best part and the reason why it made this book. While dining, we looked around at the other diners and their great dishes. Every. Single. One. Took pictures of these presentations and posted them on social media. Barton G has a captive audience paying ridiculous prices with an inconvenient process and average reviews yet everyone there is *doing their marketing for them!*

They have a marketing team I'm sure, but in this case it isn't really necessary. Every patron in there was not only posting on social media *on their behalf, free of charge*, they were also posting to their own individual uncensored profiles with a fresh new potential customer list every time. What's better is that these are all personal profiles and not business pages, so the reach is infinitely better than Barton G's own social pages! Absolute genius.

Immune to Marketing – The Holy Grail of Restaurant Success

Ya know those bars in your neighborhood that have been there since before you can remember? The ones that never advertise, probably don't even know how to post on Facebook, and have an hour wait every weekend? These places have such a good history that they have become what I call *"immune to marketing."* These places all have several constants in common. The most obvious one is a ton of crazy crap on the walls. You can tell at a glance if the place has an extensive history. If every conceivable square inch of wall space has something covering it, the place has been around the block a few decades. Most of these places have been around since before social media. They have been built on a solid platform of a few universally successful aspects. Great people, great food, or a combination of both. These places can appeal to tourists or locals alike and still be successful. Being immune to marketing takes time. And a lot of it. However, much like the fictional restaurant Shenaniganz in the movie *Waiting*, trying to manufacture this look by bolting a ton of crap on the walls but offering a watered-down chain-store experience doesn't work.

Unfortunately, when these older, authentic restaurants that have achieved this immunity to marketing try to open an additional location, rarely does it work out. These places have gotten where they are by an extensive history of doing things right. Plus a ton of luck. New locations look, well, new. Rarely does a stark white, barren, hospital-like setting work out. These additional locations often inadvertently bring on a Vegas feel—a cheap rip-off of the original. Speaking of Vegas...

Your Appeal Is Like an Over/Under Bet in Vegas

Here is something I've put way more thought into than I probably should have. When I drive long distances and zone out listening to *The Wall* for the four hundredth time, I think of shit like this. If you had to summarize your restaurant or bar's rate of success in the *"How appealing is it?"* category, keep one question in mind: *Where have you set expectations?*

Where you've set the bar is like placing an over/under wager. If you set the bar too high, customers may not see the value in your product. They may think *"Yeah, it was ok I guess, but $60 for a steak? Fuck that place!"* If you set the bar, and expectations, humbly, people may think more along the lines of *"I wasn't expecting that type of food or service from a place with no signage, a cluttered looking interior, and having* *to enter through the alley. Hell, I'm happy I found a $60 steak and an atmosphere that I actually love!"*

You're placing that bet with your design, your atmosphere, and especially your marketing. Betting the *under* will almost always win. Betting the under means being humble. Subtle. Flying under the radar. We all know places like this. Sure, they have their disadvantages but the advantages always seem to win people over.

The hard part is getting the word out before going broke, when "letting the public know how cool you are" with a big PR push and tons of marketing is betting the over.

Very often Burger King will get better reviews than a high-end steak house in the same area. The steak house has set the bar too high and didn't deliver. All Burger King has to do is open the doors. People know exactly what they're getting. They know the service is probably going to suck. They know the bathrooms are probably going to look like a scene out of *Hostel*. They know all of this and still grab lunch way more times per week than they probably should. And the online reviews reflect this.

When it comes to online reviews especially, you have two choices—set that bar high and pray you impress the shit out of people every single time or set it low and let them be pleasantly surprised. The 1-star Yelp crowd loves kicking the high-bar-setters in the balls. They cherish the entitled online privilege of being able to tell the public, *"Meh, I wasn't impressed. Not sure what all the hype is about."* But when all the hype is limited to word of mouth, and the "new restaurant in town" suggestion comes from a trusted friend instead of an Instagram post, now this Yelpite feels like he has the inside track. They bet the *under* and won this guy over.

When going out in the LA area, I saw one glaring similarity—every bar, almost *literally every bar*, is setting the bar at an all-time low, and it's genius! Pretty much every bar concept in the Hollywood area can be described as *"a throwback prohibition-era speakeasy theme"* that's super subtle, has no signage whatsoever, and you need a roadmap to find the front door. Just look for the huge dude sitting on the stool by a nondescript door in a sketchy alley. Pretty much the exact opposite of what we've been taught by traditional restaurant and bar designs of the past.

Approaching joints like this may make you feel nervous, a bit intimidated actually. But they've mastered the art of being subtle. When you go from thinking you're definitely in the wrong neighborhood after dark to having the most fun you've had in recent memory, this bar just chalked up another win by betting the under. Of course all restaurants don't have this luxury that a nightclub or bar does. Nor does the speakeasy vibe work in every market. But in ever-expanding markets across the US, flashy exterior signs and cheese-ball door greeters are losing ground to the place with the most unbelievable food served by the friendly guy who you would try to avoid in real life because of the tattoo sleeves and crazy facial hair. This guy talks to you like a friend he just met, not like an Applebee's robot. This place charges fifteen bucks per drink and no one ever bats an eye.

Authenticity Is Replacing Corporate Training

Today's savvy bar or restaurant client doesn't want to be patronized. They don't want the scripted introduction by the server. They don't want the watered-down "safe" uniforms and attitudes. I try to write with authenticity for this same reason. I could never make it through one of the hundreds of Amazon's books on restaurant marketing. They all bore the living shit out of me. They read like textbooks. The last thing we all want to do after another long-ass shift while stressing over money is to pick up a goddamn textbook! I write like I'm having a real-life one-on-one discussion. I write like I'm talking to friends. I say "fuck" a lot and write just like that. This is how human nature *enjoys* absorbing knowledge. This is how your patrons enjoy being communicated to as well. Maybe without all the fuck words, but you get the idea.

Authenticity comes across with not only attitudes but with restaurant design as well. With the exception of certain small-town markets, I predict the nationwide chains are going to start dying a slow death. Mark my words. Anything above the fast-food mark is going to come to the end of its life span. People don't want a copy/paste restaurant. In today's world of three-second attention spans, they want an authentic, unique experience.

THE MINDSET OF THE 1-STAR YELPER

We've all heard it. *"If I could give them zero stars, I would!"* I hate Yelp too. Yelp is like a kid's soccer game where the parents inevitably start fist-fighting after a questionable call from the ref. The smallest detail gone wrong will trigger the biggest, most uncalled-for and disproportional reaction. Holy shit, have I seen it all! Working in reputation management for as long as I have, you see some things. Yelp will change a man. I find myself questioning the human race quite often. I think, *"What the fuck happened to us as a species?"* I respond to reviews on behalf of my clients every single day. Then I realize these reviewers fit into a category unlike you and me.

The internet has given every pissed off kid who got picked last for middle school tag football a voice. Everyone. Pair this with today's "outrage culture," and people look forward to having a reason to complain. They *crave* it. People are dying to be able to say, *"I wasn't impressed."* They thrive on being a keyboard tough guy but run away from actual confrontation at all costs. A disturbing trend that is getting worse is the customer who has a problem but doesn't speak up so management never has an opportunity to make it right. *"How was everything?" "Great, thanks."* Then they leave a nasty note on the ticket with a justification of why they didn't tip.

Rarely does the 1-star Yelp reviewer ever give the bar or restaurant a chance to actually solve an issue they have. These days people would *actually prefer* to post a negative review than have their problem solved at the time. Hardly ever do problems get brought up and discussed with the server or bartender. Even with issues based on *taste*, another word for *opinion*. Too salty. Not hot enough. Too much ice. Too weak. Too strong. All of these are opinions but the 1-star public thinks the restaurant should know their personal preferences. There are of course universal complaints that make sense. No restaurant is perfect. We all make mistakes daily. Though these days it's more challenging than ever to please the public. Our industry is so competitive and cutthroat that, in essence, we've done it to ourselves. We can choose to improve based on the reviews. So can our competition. The weak are weeded out and close down quicker than ever. The customer service bar is so high these days that the public expects absolute perfection. Every time. No exceptions.

More times than not, the 1-star reviewer bases their review on one single experience and not an overall average. We often see the review that says something like, "*I used to go here all the time but this last visit was just horrible. Never again. 1 star!*" Even though every other experience in the past has been great.

I've seen 1-star Yelp reviews because the competing restaurant across the street was playing their music too loud. I've seen reviews where the parking garage next to the restaurant had kids who were revving their tuner cars too loud. I've seen poor reviews because they took their favorite app off the menu. I just read a 1-star review because the restaurant didn't have any A/C at the time and the complainer thought there ought to be a sign saying so, that would have made it ok. I quite often see reviews of the *crowd* and not necessarily the *business*. You know, the ones who think some guy they don't necessarily like in the bar at the same time they are is offensive in some way. "*Great place but it's full of douchebags on weekends.*" There's always the 1-star Yelp review because the reviewer wanted the TV channel changed to his game, regardless of the table of 20 guests next to him that had been there way, way before he had gotten there and were watching the game *they* came in for.

On the other side of the coin, there are also times when the restaurant had definitely, legitimately fucked up. It happens.

If you came up short and the reviewer is correct, own it and simply apologize. There's nothing wrong with a response admitting you dropped the ball during their visit. When the public reads responses, they know you're human. Humans make mistakes, just like people reading your reviews do. Don't hide behind excuses and don't get emotional. Having a professional, unemotional third-party service respond to your reviews is highly recommended. Third-party review responses remove the element of emotion from these and don't escalate the situation. Third-party responders act more like a judge and less like a lawyer. An impartial approach that gives customers the benefit of the doubt will almost always be more successful than an emotional one.

When Smart-Assery Goes Right

If you really, *really* want to grow your business and like living on the edge, consider this. If you can master the art of being a brutally honest, clever smartass, there is a huge opportunity here. We've all seen the viral news stories about a bar whose response was so honest and so over-the-top hilarious that it got shared hundreds or thousands of times over social media.

There is a sushi place here in Scottsdale called Obon. They had a 1-star Yelp review come in from a girl named Allie that mentioned something about slow service and other people getting better, quicker service than her at the time. She also mentioned it took her four hours to complete her visit, which we all know is not possible unless she chose to camp out for some reason. Believe me, Allie, no restaurant wants you camping for four hours either.

The owners of Obon have mastered the art of the brutally honest response. They basically called her out on her bullshit review and asked her to not come back. Allie then goes completely ballistic and puts her review all over social media and says she will personally pay people to write poor reviews for Obon on her behalf! I don't think anyone actually took her up on this but the fact that she went so far out of her way to trash the Obon name came off as hilarious and desperate.

Obon came back with a savagely genius response. They have a marquee sign inside the restaurant in which they quoted Allie's words on her social media account: *"I will write every review I can to ruin your business. You have no idea who you have pissed off!"* They then took it a step further and used Allie's words against her. In an ironic twist, they shared her review on *their own social media accounts*, in essence making a joke out of the whole thing.

Here is the kicker—Obon then offered a 20% discount to anyone named Allie, Al, Allison, etc. and put some money behind the post. The response was immediate. Everyone saw the humor in the petty review and actually started tagging friends whose name matched the offer. Obon was cashing in on this potentially negative situation and the buzz was enormous. Everyone had Obon's back on this one, and they were able to profit from this delicate situation. I had several people tag me on the post and bring it up in conversation. Obon had people who had never before been through the doors showing up for the offer. Others not named Allie showed up as well. Everyone can appreciate a well-positioned and clever response to an obviously entitled whiner.

Allie was never heard from again.

There can, of course, have an equal and opposite effect if this is done poorly. Also here in the Scottsdale area, just a few miles away from Obon, there was a place called Amy's Baking Company. "Was" a place. Amy's used the same response of calling out customers who didn't leave a truthful review but did it in a way that almost everyone found offensive. Her approach used a whiny, accusatory tone that came off as complaining instead of understanding. Amy's also made huge waves on social media and even made the TV news on several occasions. All reports added more nails to Amy's coffin in this case. The food was actually damn good but when everyone dislikes the owners on a personal level *that much*, the doors were inevitably closing. Amy's never recovered and went under shortly after this. Her restaurant was even featured on Kitchen Nightmares with Gordon Ramsey and was one of the few places Gordon walked away from. He refused to work with her.

Putting people on blast first requires that you are 100% factually correct. As mentioned earlier, if you dropped the ball to any degree, maybe skip a snarky response to that one. Next make sure there is a certain amount of humor in your response so you don't come off defensive. If the author of the review is simply not your demographic and should have managed their expectations prior to showing up at your business in the first place, maybe mention this as well. *"You walked into a dirty dive bar called 'Shooters,' what exactly did you think you would find here? We apologize for the lack of white tablecloths even though this is the first time we've had this complaint in our 20-year history."*

In the cases where these responses are used correctly and humorously, they are well worth the 1-star review. Look up *Thruster's Lounge* in San Diego on Yelp—their responses are priceless! As of this writing, Yelp has a big red banner across their page that says, *"This business is being monitored by Yelp's support team for content related to media reports."* They've received so many positive reviews to support them based on their hilarious review responses that Yelp actually had to step in and suspend further reviews on their page! One of their responses mentioned something like, *"Do you really expect 5-star service from a bar who literally has a dildo as a tap handle?"* This is accurate. There are pictures of this on Yelp. Well done, Thrusters. They couldn't have paid for exposure like this if they tried.

To wrap this up, I hope the days of the unanswered reviews are behind us. By now we know the importance of responding to every single online review, good or bad. Respond quickly and honestly. Never, *ever* copy/paste responses. If you can grab some well-deserved media exposure, then take advantage of that shit! We should be paying *very* close attention to these reviews. Your new potential customers sure as hell are.

Build a Better Mousetrap

You've probably heard of these systems out there that you may have been pitched from marketing guys about *"promoting good reviews"* and *"preventing poor reviews."* This is where a piece of software or some other method will reach out to your customers via email, text, or whatever and ask the customer to leave a review within these internal review systems. The idea is that positive reviews will come in, which prompts the customer to "share" the review on a legit review platform like Google, Yelp, or Facebook. Conversely, negative reviews are theoretically retained internally so we have a chance to field them and make this customer happy *before* they end up as a 1-star Yelp review. This is called "Review Mousetrapping." Great theory, bad result.

Human nature does not follow this process. I used similar systems for years and even helped develop one for use within a Wi-Fi marketing tool. This idea of "preventing bad reviews" makes restaurant owners salivate just thinking about it. In reality, when the public gets these emails saying something like, *"How did we do? Please rate your experience,"* they are suddenly reminded to go on Yelp and kick us in the virtual nuts if they had a poor experience instead of using this internal system.

Very few reviews come in via this process compared to traditional review sites. I've used all methods and all different approaches to asking for these reviews. What's worse is that if people do use this system and write a positive review, *very rarely* do they "click through" and paste their great review on a site like Yelp or Google. This rate has dropped even further in recent years to damn near zero. The jig is up and the public knows exactly what is going on behind the scenes. Like I mentioned, today's consumers don't want their issues resolved, they *want* to complain to others online. They know their personal opinion won't ever get out there to cyberspace if this internal system is used. So they ignore it.

Again, this is my personal, very unpopular opinion. Other "marketing specialists" will most definitely tell you I'm crazy and I'm just not doing it right. They'll wow you with huge impressive-sounding statistics and anecdotal case studies about how this one time, this one restaurant was able to double their numbers using this system alone! It's doubtful this ever happened in real life, even back ten or so years ago when these mousetrapping systems first started showing up and were sort of relevant. This opinion is obviously not good for business for someone like me who is in the restaurant marketing business but, hell, I'd rather stick to the truth.

THE "IT" FACTOR

I've said it many times before. If there was a formula for restaurant and bar success that I could publish and sell, I'd be a gazillionaire. Success requires several common-sense ingredients you are well aware of, so I won't bore you with those. What we don't really ever discuss is the *it* factor. The restaurant that has *it* will succeed. The ones that don't will struggle or fail.

Just like celebrities or musicians, either you have *it*, or you don't. My favorite examples of the *it* factor are Apple products. I'm a Samsung/PC guy personally. The iPhone, in my very unpopular opinion, is an inferior product. I used to have both an iPhone and a Samsung Galaxy for different businesses and used them both at the same time for a while. The iPhone was slower, harder to deal with, unnecessarily complicated, way harder to type on, and for some reason it seemed like it asked for my goddamn Apple password every time I tried doing anything.

I found the same frustrations with the iMac, which I also owned for a brief amount of time until I about threw that fucking thing out the window of a moving car. I gave them both a chance but found all Apple products insanely frustrating and poorly designed.

I started asking people who had an iPhone or an iMac why they preferred Apple products. Most of the time they would mention some random app—which was also available on a Samsung (or any other phone, for that matter). Or they would mention being able to sync all of their documents and passwords across all browsers and folders (also available on any phone, browser, or computer). Rarely is there a rational reason mentioned. Furthermore, when something inevitably breaks on an Apple product, you can't just walk into an Apple store and get some help. You have to make an appointment online, which could potentially be weeks out!

When I keep pressing the iPhone/iMac crowd as to their preference for an inferior, more expensive product, they would eventually just say, *"I don't know, I just like them, leave me alone!"* What Apple products lack in usability, affordability, and simplicity, they make up in sex appeal. In spades. Apple products don't have to be reliable. Or easy to deal with. Or compatible with other non-Apple products. They are damn cool looking, and looks go a long way with today's consumers.

Apple has perfected a sexy, appealing aesthetic that speaks to one's heart, not their brain. People have an *emotional* response to Apple's products. As bar and restaurant operators, if we can capture a small piece of what Apple has perfected, we will be monumentally successful. When a consumer can't quite tell you *why* they prefer a certain restaurant or bar, but they instinctively return again and again, *that* is the formula for success. That is the *it* factor.

The emotional response obviously has to include the basics. Great food, great service, and a good atmosphere. What really taps into people's emotions are the subtleties like lighting, temperature, smell, colors, noise volume, music choices, and other factors that are hugely important but to which some operators may not pay much attention. I don't have all of the specific answers here but do yourself a favor and hire a designer that specializes in restaurant design and ambiance. If they know what they're doing, it will always be money well spent.

Possibly the Most Competitive Nightlife Market in America

The Scottsdale, Arizona, entertainment district is the perfect testing grounds for the *it* factor. It consists of a T-shaped road, all of about 50 yards long. There are thirteen bars and clubs back-to-back along this road. The highest-grossing dollar-per-square-foot bars in Arizona are all in this area. There are clubs here doing 6M per year with about 3500 sq. ft. of public space. There are also clubs *directly next door* to the successful ones that struggle to keep the doors open with more than twice the space. The tight concentration of clubs all competing for the same customer makes this entertainment district the most competitive environment I've ever seen in the nightlife industry. More than Miami, more than Vegas, more than LA.

What seems even more strange is the fact that all of these clubs are carbon copies of each other. There are nuances that set them slightly apart but the big picture is almost identical. They all consist of rectangular rooms with smaller rectangular bars in the center, roll up doors which open to the outside air, and plenty of booths for bottle service. The incestuous staff also seem to migrate from one club to the next to the next when something doesn't work out. So the people are all identical as well.

Drink prices in this area are high, yet identical. The consumer experience is pretty much the same from one bar to the next. The DJs all play a similar mix of Top 40 and EDM. The pretty people don't necessarily flock to one bar over the next, but they are in abundance on this block. The places that serve food serve pretty much the same options and quality as the place next door. People just seem to go where the rest of the people are. Nothing attracts a crowd like a crowd.

Egos of the successful bar owners are as high as the bewilderment of the owners of the failing bars right next door. Location is rule number 1, 2, and 3, BUT the *it* factor is a close 4. The successful bars all have some common factors but there are exceptions here as well. The clubs managed by the "cool kids" seem to be more successful. This goes for their promoters as well. The higher volume of customers attracts the better-looking female bartenders. These Insta-famous girls seem to be a required element of success in the area.

Quite a few of these places have several theme parties per week. When I used to have access to the Facebook and Instagram analytics and was involved with theme parties for several of these clubs, I noticed the law of diminishing returns kicked in quickly, if not immediately. Theme parties are expensive and lose their value completely if used too often. Once or twice a month is ok, but two to three per week is ridiculous. These require a person to plan the event, a costume organizer to dress the staff and decorate the club, a graphic designer to make a flyer, a video editor to make a quick promotional video clip, a promotions team to get the word out, a social media manager to post it online, and a management team at the club to execute. This is a huge undertaking! And costly.

When I started asking the bartenders I worked with at these clubs how the public was responding to them, they used their robotic knee-jerk response and said, *"They're awesome, everyone loves them!"* Then I explained I'm not looking for a "team-player" response. I asked for the truth. I was not asking to have someone else justify the job I was doing. I wanted the *actual* truth. Since I asked *like that*, the truth came flowing out like they were releasing a ton of bricks off their backs. They would instantly change their tune and explain that, no offense, but no one cares or even knows that these events were planned. None taken!

They would go on to say that more times than not, the public would show up, look them up and down, and ask why they were all dressed up in Halloween costumes. They would explain the theme party of the night. Customers would reply with somewhat of an "oh, ok" and order a drink. Customers were supposed to dress up to match these themes but they rarely, if ever, did. The only value I could see was that the customers out on the street would walk in once in a while to see what all the crap hanging from the ceiling was all about. This sometimes resulted in a few sales but never enough to justify the ongoing weekly expense to throw these parties. The daily numbers would rarely reflect an increase based on a theme party. Yet the parties continue. Multiple parties per week continue to this day in this environment.

I got the feeling that certain owners preferred the artificial "hype" to successfully increasing business. Again, egos are at Everest proportions here.

So WHY such huge differences in bottom line numbers with such similar bars and customer experiences? Sometimes the advantages are things you can't put your finger on. Something unmeasurable. Or maybe the successful bars in this area do things 1% better in each category. When these categories are all added up, it equals a great base crowd. Which attracts an even bigger crowd. Which makes all the difference in the world.

Maybe it's just the invisible, indefinable *it* factor?

MENU SCIENCE

I'll keep this one brief since chances are you've heard the basics before. This is where a lot of places leave money on the table. You just spent statistically $40–$80 in marketing dollars to get that new person in the door. Maximizing spend and profit margin is the next crucial step. Menu science can get as boring as SEO if I get too in depth, so we'll stick with the basics. The menu's job is to steer people into ordering what YOU want them to order, not just provide a list of items that you offer. Boxing or highlighting one item in each category will increase orders of that product by up to 30%. The *"Chef's Specials"* that we've all seen may not necessarily be something the chef is good at; it's more than likely the highest-profit-margin item in that category.

One thing that I've seen emerging more and more are bold statements like, *"We dare you to find better wings than ours! If you don't agree these are the best wings you've ever had, they're free!"* Chances are if a customer didn't like something they ordered, you'd comp it anyway, so this sounds risky but really isn't. Just make SURE you have the best wings anywhere before trying out this one.

In today's viral online world, if your "challenge" is interesting or outrageous enough, it can create a huge buzz. When people start to take photos of it and post them to social media, you now have people marketing this challenge for you. For free. If something like this goes viral on a national level, this alone can bring people in the doors for months or even years.

Remember "*The ol' 96'r*" porterhouse steak challenge in the movie *The Great Outdoors*? So does everyone else.

THE PROCESS OF MAKING THE DINING DECISION

I mentioned the *"Fishbowl vs. The Ocean"* concept previously and in great detail in my last book, so I'll keep it brief. The Fishbowl consists of your current customers and people who are familiar with your business. Social media, email databases, text message clubs all fall under this category. But what about the tourists and people who are new to the area who have no idea you exist? They reside in the Ocean. Google, Yelp, and TripAdvisor are available to all consumers and, like it or not, your business resides here as well. Here is the insane part—most marketing budgets focus entirely inside the Fishbowl so the tourist looking for a great burger or beer will never find you. Business does not evolve exclusively inside the Fishbowl of existing customers. The huge strides forward are in the Ocean.

Let's look at our own consumer habits. When in unfamiliar territory or venturing outside your comfort zone, ask *yourself* what tools you use to find a place to eat or drink when *you* are a tourist. Remember—you are way more in tune and familiar with restaurants around your hometown, so let's leave that area out of this equation. Let's say you're in a tourist town like Las Vegas and are not familiar with the lay of the land, and we'll assume you don't have any hook-ups or any history of visits.

Chances are if you ask a hotel employee or concierge, they will be forced to promote only the restaurants owned by the parent company of the hotel or "partner" businesses. Not a very impartial selection. The next choice is to grab that little computer in your pocket. What now? The Yelp app and Google top the list. International consumers will tend to gravitate to TripAdvisor. *Social media accounts for about 4% of the go-to apps in this case.* Again, you can't follow someone you don't know exists. In this scenario, you are the tourist swimming aimlessly in the Ocean.

Human nature usually starts with one of these apps and then, if necessary, the user may click over to Instagram and do some more research on a particular restaurant before making a decision. Like I mentioned earlier, if the conversation comes up with the server about how the customer found them, a picture on their Instagram page may be mentioned. Then mentally that server is thinking that Instagram brought that party through the door when in reality, without Google, they never would have seen the Instagram page in the first place. Instagram and Facebook have moved to research tools almost exclusively in cases like this. Yelp, TripAdvisor, and Google are the *catalysts*. When creating a marketing plan for your restaurant, if you don't take the catalyst seriously, the rest of the steps consumers will take to find you online won't ever have happen.

A Good Staff Is Hard to Find – What I learned in Mexico

With today's younger, entitled population entering the workforce, finding people who don't mind hustling and doing hard, rewarding work is getting tougher and tougher. Luckily, most restaurant employees still work on an effort-vs-reward system: tips. Human nature dictates that if more effort is put forth, the reward should follow. All entrepreneurs and business owners fall into this category as well. (Although in this case, the risk and struggle is guaranteed, the reward is not.) On a recent trip to Sayulita, Mexico, I noticed almost all of the locals "worked for themselves" or sold goods and services without anyone over them forcing them to produce. Anyone from beach vendors to bartenders all have a hustler's attitude and were genuinely trying their best to make sales and make tourists happy. They were only accountable to themselves. If they didn't produce, their income directly suffered that day. On the other hand, in an employer/ salaried employee relationship, the employee gets paid no matter if they provide results or not. This structure produces complacency and laziness.

As a side-note, I now know why Americans have an international reputation for being assholes. We have raised the bar so high recently in America that countries like Mexico seem like they are failing. In reality they are right where we were not too long ago, if not ahead of us. Now that we have an ever-growing atmosphere of "virtual word

of mouth" (online reviews), we are forced to get better and better in order to stay relevant. Sure, Mexico has TripAdvisor, but they don't seem to obsess over negative reviews like we do. Americans are so used to top-notch food and service that they take it for granted until they get out of this near-perfect environment. I often see Americans sitting at a Mexican bar beside me losing their minds because their food is taking upwards of an hour. Yes, hour ticket times are common in Mexico and, honestly, no one down there seems to give a fuuuuuuuuck if you think that's too long. It's not from understaffing. It's not from being lazy. That's just how Mexico operates. When Americans try to apply our standards to other countries is when it gets ugly. And we start to get a reputation.

Anyway, if it's at all possible, tips should be shared among the staff with everyone from the kitchen staff to every other low-paying position being included. The worst thing to do is to take away their incentive to produce. I recently read an online review of a fast-casual restaurant where management, according to the reviewer, kept all of the tips. Judging by the environment and the average ticket, this probably didn't amount to much—for a business owner. The meager amount in the tip jar meant the owners could maybe buy themselves a quick lunch with what was left. Those few additional bucks per day meant a considerable bit more to a young counter person or server making barely enough to make rent, even with the help of their other two jobs. Believe me, I used to be one of them.

Don't get me wrong, I'm not going on some Bernie Sanders "this isn't fair" rant. Quite the opposite. I held three jobs as a youngster in my 20s and barely squeaked by even with the help of two other roommates packed into a shithole apartment in Utah. It was just life back then. No one complained about it. No one marched in the streets. No one held rallies. Life back in the 90s was just as "unfair" as it is now. Maybe back then we were all just a bit tougher? I was having the time of my life actually. There's something special about that time of your life when everything you own fits in the back of your pickup.

One of my jobs was bussing tables and washing dishes at a tourist-heavy restaurant on main street in Park City, UT. I usually walked with about $13–$15 in tips per shift, but damn if I didn't look forward to that tip-out every night I worked! Management considered changing the format and not tipping out the bussers and the kitchen staff. There was damn near a mutiny when this was discussed. I quit that gig before this came to be a reality as it was my own tiny slice of happiness at the end of a slam-packed night washing *way* too many dishes. Pair this with constantly broken equipment and an environment that was always hovering around 90% humidity because the dish room wasn't properly ventilated, and you've got a long-ass night. My shoes would be soaked through to the bone and my feet sore as hell from standing on the slippery-ass, greasy tile instead of a mat. Apparently that wasn't in the budget. This was before heading home at 2 am in the minus-10-degree Utah winter.

That 13 to 15 Buck Tip-out at the End of the Night Made It All Worth Doing

So again, if at all possible, share tips with your staff. All of your staff. And whatever you do, if there is a tip jar that goes to management instead of the counter staff, stop that shit immediately. You're not only destroying morale, you're hurting your business. The pennies you save will never amount to the damage done by shitty attitudes and a staff who secretly despises you.

Today's hourly or salary office employees laughably describe "working your ass off" as putting in your eight hours of work and sometimes a little overtime. But how many of those eight hours are productive?

Did the company make money during that entire time? Was the goal to be successful and reach goals before walking out for the day? Or was it to log those eight hours with roughly 40% work and 60% bullshitting with your co-worker about their football picks, then running for the door at 5:01? Don't get me wrong, I'm not bashing the hourly or salary worker. I did it for the majority of my life. There is nothing wrong with that position if you prefer guaranteed pay over unlimited growth potential. But it is the opposite of what you'd refer to as "motivational."

When I logged my time at corporate offices working at restaurant marketing departments, I saw this firsthand for decades. "Going through the motions" was what they all did, often myself included. If we could get the job done in an hour but had all day to finish the job, damn right we'd make sure and drag that shit out for eight hours. We got paid no matter how productive we were. Or weren't. If you have the opportunity, substitute a partial tipped/bonus position for straight salary. When the drive to succeed has its rewards, things tend to get done. Way quicker and way better.

WHAT IF? A COMPLETELY NEW RESTAURANT MODEL WAS CREATED...

What if we changed how everything was done? I mean everything. We've established that repeat customers are built from great consumer experiences. Then they are multiplied by great online reviews and word of mouth. The two biggest complaints leading to poor reviews and negative word of mouth are, of course, bad food and bad service. Chances are, like me, most people reading this book were once servers, bartenders, or worked in the kitchen. We most likely hated our jobs and barely tolerated them. We also put out just enough effort to not get fired. A D-minus performance was good enough for us. The reason? *"I don't get paid enough for this shit!"*

But What If We Did?

With labor taking up a huge majority of the expense of operating a bar or restaurant, you may say there isn't any room to pay another dime for salary or hourly employees. Owners or managers will say (to themselves of course), *"We don't have another ounce of "give-a-fuck" to pour into these employees who don't really appreciate us anyway."* And this same model goes on and on for another 50 years or so…

Let's think about roadblocks to success logically. Paying *slightly better* than your competition is all it may take. Management will have to be pretty tight and goal orientated as well. When all employees share in the better income and advantages that this particular restaurant offers, everyone wins. With better pay, we get better employees. We can pick and choose the best of the best instead of hiring warm bodies to go through the motions. Better-paid management hires better-paid employees. Better-paid employees produce a better customer experience. Feeling your value and getting paid more than your job description usually pays feels good. Feeling good leads to better attitudes and all employees will have an added incentive to bring more to the table.

So get out of the mindset of *"They don't really deserve it because my employees don't do that great of a job."*

Get into the mindset of *"I can offer better pay and afford the best out there. The best will help multiply business and success for all of us."*

- Better pay = better employees.
- Better employees = a better consumer experience.
- A better consumer experience = positive word of mouth and better online reviews.
- Better online reviews **multiply** business, they don't just add to it.

As we've discussed, the top three biggest factors in building *new* business and capturing the undecided customer are word of mouth, online reviews, and Google. By a long shot. Don't add customers the old-fashioned way by adding one at a time. *Multiply* them by leveraging a happy staff. Statistically, a single 1-star review can cost your place 30 customers! The traditional cost of customer acquisition is about $60 per customer. So if a single 1-star review can cost you the equivalent of $1800 in marketing dollars, what is it worth now to pay your staff a slightly-higher-than-market-value price? Pretty simple really! And that's based on only *one* negative online review or poor customer experience.

With a happy, well-paid staff, turnover is greatly reduced. Staff training isn't quite as common. Sick days and no-call/no-shows are cut down dramatically. With better attitudes come better tips, so a lot of this increased income isn't even paid by the restaurant. You can now tap into a slightly more professional, more mature, more aesthetically-looking pool of people to employ. We've all heard about the fine-dining servers in Manhattan who make well into the six-figure range and have been waiting tables their whole life. This is possible anywhere, it just takes rethinking the entire restaurant and bar industry.

Offering the same pay and same environment as your competition will attract the same ol' employees that they have. When you offer the best to your employees, you have an unfair advantage over everyone.

Remember, *you* don't dictate your online reviews or drive business through word of mouth, your staff does.

What We Can Learn from the Car Industry.

Another possible model would be to pay your staff like car dealers get paid, by using a Customer Satisfaction Index (CSI). If you've ever bought a new car, salespeople often ask—well, beg, really—to have you give them *"all 10s."* After your purchase you will receive a survey in the mail asking how your purchase experience went. Their pay, and possibly their job, depends on these high marks. Bad marks can often lead to anything from write-ups to being fired. On a bigger scale, the dealership may even lose its ability to sell cars if this gets bad enough.

According to Edmunds.com:

> *"Customer Satisfaction Index (CSI) scores are an important part of everyday life at a dealership, and for good reason. Automakers want*

to hear from customers in order to gauge how well the franchise is doing in key areas, primarily customer satisfaction with the sales process. On the dealership level, these scores often determine future inventory. The better the score, the more likely a dealership is to get in-demand vehicles. Depending on the manufacturer, CSI scores also can affect the quarterly or annual bonuses it pays to the dealership, which are often essential to the dealership's bottom line."

What if…

…restaurants adopted this model? Employees would receive bonuses based on star ratings, online reviews, and repeat customers. Yes, this would be a bit tough to track but with the technology at our fingertips, there are several online loyalty apps that can make this easy. Imagine both the FOH and kitchen staff being paid on this index. No more chef blaming the servers and vice-versa. We succeed or fail together, and get paid accordingly.

What if…

…the manager, *not the server*, brings the check to the table and asks how the service was? If the server does a bad job, the guest is almost *never* going to speak up to the very server who showed them this shitty service. They will be way more likely, however, to speak up to a manager who drops off the check. There is no other factor existing today that will curb negative online reviews better than this!

What if…

…the manager then asks, "Is there anything about your visit that would prevent a 5-star review?" This is the point where tight-lipped guests may speak up and mention something they normally wouldn't. We, of course, don't want to solicit reviews or offer rewards for positive reviews. Asking for honest feedback is becoming necessary, and much appreciated. The future of your business relies on this.

Again, now you are multiplying business instead of just adding to it.

Building a Slow Day into a Successful One.

One of the first things I hear when consulting with a new client is their drive to "fill in the gaps" in a slow week. I briefly discussed this in my first book. Just because you build it, doesn't mean they will come. Not unless you are tapping into an existing market.

During slow times, the common thought process is to offer drink or food specials or create other motivational means to bringing business through the door. We sometimes get the bottom feeders and the Groupon-ers at best. More often we get nothing. Motivating someone to get off the couch and drive down to your restaurant is tough as hell. People don't leave the house for specials or slightly cheaper food. They don't leave the house for gimmicky events or contests. What they will do, however, is leave the bar a few doors down and come to yours for the right reason.

If there is a pool of existing customers near you, tapping into this market is infinitely easier and cheaper than trying to create a market where it doesn't exist. Chances are, you know who's killing it on a Tuesday near you. You probably know why they are doing great as well. Maybe they do have cheap as hell drinks. Maybe it's a bar themed toward a certain football team who is coincidentally doing great that year. Maybe it's the oldest trick in the book like a wet T-shirt contest or some sort of bikini-clad wrestling. Either way, if there is an existing market that you simply aren't capturing yet, it can be yours. Just make sure you don't make the mistake of trying to rip-off what the competition is doing with a basic plan to do it "better." What actually happens is that the public will see it for what it is—a cheap rip-off of the original. These ill-conceived plans rarely, if ever, work out.

So if your competition is doing a college-themed night with a college crowd, do something completely different that will appeal to a college crowd. It must be bigger and better in all aspects. Get creative and create a buzz. Make the description of the night something that, when explained, will cause people to stop and say, *"Wait, what the hell are they doing? I gotta go check that out!"* These could be as easy as Goldfish Races, Stoplight Parties, Tinder-based games, or other "been done" events. The truly great ones, however, haven't necessarily been done before. Just make sure you have an existing pool of customers in close proximity from which to pull. Be a pioneer and make that shit happen!

THE STORY OF FIREBALL WHISKY

Before Fireball Cinnamon Whisky exploded into the national brand it is today, it came from modest roots. With a little simple-yet-genius marketing in place, it grew bigger than Jägermeister in just under a few years. Depending on who you talk to, the story goes something like this:

Fireball started out as Dr. McGillicuddy's Fireball Cinnamon Whisky, which boasted a super old-school snake-oil-looking label reminiscent of the 1800s sketchy medicinal bottles. In 2007, the Sazerac Company bought the brand and started a marketing campaign with success almost unmatched still today. Dr. McGillicuddy's original flavor was clear in color and boring in labeling. They changed up the look of the cinnamon flavor to be bright orange with a big-ass dragon breathing fire on the label. A far cry from the cartoon-looking meteor thing they previously used.

Even though they call it "whisky" (since it's from Canada, the "e" is absent in the spelling) its formula is dangerously close to schnapps, which is where the entire Dr. McGillicuddy line came from. No self-respecting dude over eighteen years old drinks schnapps, so they had to "tweak" the recipe just enough to be able to call it whisky. It has a mere 66 proof, well under the accepted whisky minimum of 80 proof.

Fireball is thick, syrupy, and brutally hangover-inducing because of the high sugar content. Whisky (or whiskey) purists consider Fireball to be the Nickelback of the booze world and wouldn't be caught dead consuming this child's swill best suited for frat parties.

So how did an alcohol brand skyrocket to success like it did? According to Fireball's Wikipedia page, *"It's also one of the most successful liquor brands in decades. In 2011, Fireball accounted for a mere $1.9 million in sales in U.S. gas stations, convenience stores, and supermarkets, according to IRI, a Chicago-based market research firm. In 2013, sales leapt to $61 million, passing Jameson Irish whiskey and Patrón tequila."* How did something that tastes like liquid sugar, with such a low alcohol content, masquerading as whisky, surpass sales of Jägermeister, Jameson, and Patron?

Marketing

The marketing minds behind Fireball identified both their exact customer and a gap in the market and capitalized brilliantly. The label was updated to speak to the inner nine-year-old-boy of every American male out there, and since it was technically "whisky," their manhood could stay intact. Could you imagine a country music song that mentioned, *"That Fireball Schnapps whispers temptation in my ear?"* They would promptly be laughed out of Nashville. BUT... Changing one word makes it acceptable to young guys and girls across the country. Suddenly they're not kids sneaking a sip from their parents' liquor cabinet, they are adults drinking "the hard stuff!"

Before Fireball was a household name—and since it's a pretty hard sale without a little explanation—their marketing team kicked it old school and hit the streets in a grass-roots campaign. They won over bartenders one at a time in college towns across the US. Word of mouth helped spread the brand's recognition. When Fireball made it into several country music songs, it was curtains for the competition.

Ask yourself if you are capitalizing on your exact customer. Are you exploiting a gap in the market that no one else noticed? Are you providing goods or services that no one else offers? Or is your restaurant/bar providing yet another similar option in the sea of available bars in your area? Be that whisky in a sea of schnapps!

MARKETING THE LIVE MUSIC EXPERIENCE

Before we get ahead of ourselves, let's make sure we're walking perfectly before we decide to start running. A well-oiled operations machine is needed before we start bringing the crowds in the door. If operations isn't firing on all cylinders, additional marketing will only let people know you suck, only quicker.

Back when I was coming up in the marketing field and learning the ropes, I was a "do what I'm told" type of employee. I started to realize that operations at the place I was working at the time was a complete clusterfuck. We had all of the classic cliché issues, from management banging the staff to drinking on the job to theft. The list goes on and on. This particular place was a country music themed bar with a musician's name that you've heard of on the sign out front. It was also a pretty big music venue that brought in some great artists who were, back then, either on their way up or on their way back down. The A-list country musicians were out of reach for anything other than the bigger stadiums. Today a lot of the artists who played at this place are household names.

We booked the bigger names when we could. We promoted the hell out of the event and gave away tickets over the airwaves via the local country music radio station. We pumped up the show to be as big of a deal as humanly possible. Bringing crowds in droves was never an issue with this place. Not pissing off half the public when they showed up was.

The building's capacity was around 1000, but we would routinely pack in 1500+. When the bar is five deep with six wells under 20,000 sq. ft. of building, it becomes damn near impossible to get a drink. People would start to realize they had to order two rounds at a time because the next time they would get the bartender's attention could be hours later. To make this worse, the owner held customer service as a last priority, and when a problem came up he would often just say, *"Fuck 'em."* At the time when the bar was at its peak, he honestly didn't need any additional business. But with an attitude like that, peak times will be short-lived. And, boy, were they.

This attitude caused a cancer in the entire staff that grew like political opinions on social media. The negativity extended into the kitchen, the door staff, and of course the FOH staff. One-star Yelp reviews were ignored or laughed at, so of course business started to drop off sharply. Tips followed suit. Attitudes got worse and the beginning-of-the-end was upon us. Operations began to pressure the marketing department to bring the people back in. This of course multiplied the negative effects. The more people we brought through the door, the quicker these people would realize we really, really sucked at providing favorable, positive experiences. When sales started slipping and new music venues started springing up, no amount of marketing could fix this downward spiral.

At the time that I left this company, I was in charge of marketing thirteen locations. When the house of cards started tumbling, I was on my way out. At the time, I alone was the entire marketing department for all thirteen locations. I didn't have a staff of people helping me. I was the web designer. I was the graphic designer. I was also the video editor, the social media manager, and the SEO guy. I booked the bands and advanced the shows. When I left I was replaced by six different people… and six different salaries. A few years after my resignation, they were down to one location, which is also closed today.

So the moral of the story is, no amount of marketing can dig you out of the hole caused by a poor customer experience. A bad reputation is a killer. If the operations department is not solid, don't waste your money on marketing. Marketing is a multiplier. It's a better idea to multiply positive experiences, not 1-star Yelp reviews.

Live Music Venues

Speaking of live music, offering a live-band performance comes with its own set of problems that could also lead to the demise of the business, only quicker. Adding live music is supposed to enhance the busy times and keep the crowd there longer to increase the average spend. If you can get the ticket price at the door to cover the cost of the band, the rest is gravy. You get to serve drinks to a packed house for full price. Sounds like what our dreams were made of back around the time we all turned 21. Here is the pour-a-bucket-of-water-on-your-face-while-you're-sleeping reality of housing live music acts.

The PA system either has to be bought up front or rented each time. The PA consists of the speakers, monitors, amplifiers, sound board, mixers, sound management system, and miles of wiring to tie all of this together. A decent PA could easily run you hundreds of thousands of dollars. If you skimp here, bands could be reluctant to play because a cheap-ass system doesn't make them sound very good. Let's be honest, the band is only playing there so they can increase their following until the real money starts rolling in anyway. A shitty PA doesn't help. If this is rented, the cost could be as little as a few hundred bucks for a small acoustic act or thousands per performance even for a "good enough" system. And this cost has to be repeated every performance.

After the PA comes backline. Backline is all of the other "stuff sitting on the stage" involved with putting on a bigger full-band show. Mics, mic stands, additional amplifiers, additional monitors, bass rigs, drum sets, and the like all add up as well. Some local touring bands may have all of this but major headlining artists who can pack a 1000-person venue most likely do not, especially if they're flying in. They will likely request top-of-the-line shit and secure it in writing via the legally binding contract so you can't cheap-out later.

Promoting live music is the aspect where marketing doesn't follow the rules I've set forth so far. This is where paid social media shines. Now we're promoting entertainment, not food and drink, so the rules have changed. Paid Facebook and Instagram ads work wonders here, contrary to what I've said in the past regarding marketing rules for your average restaurant. Now you can target fans of the band and fans of a specific music genre in your area. If the act has a big enough following, you'll have a built-in audience right out of the gate. Do *not* think that organic posts will reach their fans, however! This is where paying for a targeted reach is essential.

Acquiring talent is equally expensive and frustrating. Local acts will be knocking down your door trying to get a date to play, yet these acts usually don't have much of a following (or much to bring to the table). *"We can bring 100 or so people in the door"* means five people will show up to see them specifically. This is called a "draw." Artists with a draw bring their own crowd with them. Bigger national acts have a huge draw but are often times so expensive that the numbers don't make any sense. Local "house" acts can be good as an opener for a bigger act or to keep a crowd there longer but don't rely on them to bring people in the door. Local "original artists" unfortunately have the smallest draw and rarely keep a crowd. They play their own songs that pretty much no one in the place, with the exception of the five people they brought with them, has ever heard of. This is where the "artistic" aspect breaks down. This catch-22 is where the artist's frustration lies. Be a soulless cover band but actually get gigs and entertain the crowd. Or be an original artist and hardly ever get a gig anywhere.

Good-quality cover bands can keep a crowd, especially if they play to a specific genre, dress the part, and make a visual impact as well. Check out Metalhead in the Phoenix, Arizona, area. These guys are a great example of a heavy metal band who play covers successfully. Metalhead has had weekly gigs in the valley for decades and remained one of the longest-running acts in the Phoenix valley until recently. You cannot miss the ripped jeans, dirty, often offensive T-shirts, spikes, and hair teased to the ceiling like a Sunset Strip band circa 1987. They are awesome at what they do and extremely entertaining. But they are not "artists" in the traditional sense of the word. They play exclusively heavy metal covers and there is a good likelihood that you know the words to every one of the songs they play.

If you have enough capacity to be able to justify a huge national act, you'll have to get familiar with dealing with talent agencies and lengthy contracts. These are the bands in the $20k-$40k and up range. In my experience, if you break even at the door, you're doing pretty good with a band of this caliber. Meaning your income from tickets sold will equal the price you had to pay to get this band to play. I won't get into a "guarantee" as opposed to a "versus," deal which splits the door money with the band. Do a quick Google search if you're interested in how to structure a deal like this.

All contracts and requests are negotiable. You have the right to redline the shit out of a live music contract, especially the boilerplate contracts provided by the big agencies like William Morris or CAA. This goes for the "rider" as well. The rider is the list of sometimes ridiculous crap that bands will try to get you to provide them. The notorious "No brown M&M's" story was written into Van Halen's rider to make sure the talent buyer was actually reading the whole rider. Van Halen's contract said that if there were any brown M&M's anywhere backstage, the venue forfeits the entire agreed-upon price and the band doesn't have to perform. It was actually inserted to make sure the venue was paying attention to contractual details from a safety aspect and no paragraph was glossed over. However, I suspect the band expected this to get screwed up from time to time and could then justify trashing a green room.

Oftentimes, a 40 line-item rider can be redlined in its entirety and replaced with "We will provide two bottles of liquor of your choice and dinner for eight people." Riders should be deemed as a request, not a requirement.

This all sounds amazing and makes for some great street cred if a huge show is pulled off successfully. With every advantage is a list of disadvantages in this industry. The biggest unwanted side effect of offering live music is pigeonholing yourself as *only* a music venue. If your crowd refuses to show up unless there is a band playing, you have a whole new set of problems. There are quite a few venues across the country that are just that—exclusively venues. No cheeseburgers. No happy hour. Just a place to buy a drink and watch a band. If you are a bar or restaurant first and a live music venue second, people may assume there isn't anything going on during the nights a band isn't booked. Like a cliché junkie-musician of the 80s, if this happens, you could quickly slide into a necessary addiction to live music. If you book it, they will come. If you don't, you're dead on a Friday night.

"Advancing a show" means you also have to provide a person who will meet the band there, usually prior to opening. This employee is the go-to guy on the venue's side and the guy who often gets yelled at if something goes sideways. He's the guy who shows the band where to set up, where the green room is (if there is one), gets them fed, and pays them at the end of the performance. Expenses pile up quickly for live performances.

Live music is fun and exciting if you are set up for success. It makes for the hardest and longest nights that you'll actually enjoy. It's where the legendary *"I was there"* stories originate from. It can be profitable but the odds are stacked against you. In an industry where breaking even is considered a win, there is a very good chance that long-term costs will outweigh profit. If you want to have an acoustic guitar player for happy hour, do it, but limit it to that unless you know what you're signing up for.

LAST CALL

The main takeaway from this book should be to use common sense and draw your own conclusions. Don't rely on "marketing experts" who may possibly know less than you already know. If a certain technique or process goes against human nature, it's probably bullshit. Apply your own behavior when you are a tourist to acquiring new customers for your restaurant. When in unfamiliar areas, chances are you use the three major tools of the undecided customer—Google, Yelp, and TripAdvisor. Keep in mind no one knows the market in your own neighborhood better than you. Even though you would never use these tools in your own backyard doesn't mean the rest of the public won't.

"Social media experts" are usually only pros at knowing *their own* habits. If you hire a 21-year-old to manage your marketing approach, your demographic had better also be the 21- to 24-year-old customer. These "experts" often apply their own personal habits and opinions to your business so the younger person's approach will most likely fail if your target customer is 35+ and you manage a fine-dining restaurant. I've seen way too many of these "experts" assume that their own online behavior translates to everyone else's. When was the last time you heard a 45-year-old man bring up someone's kick-ass Instagram stories?

Your marketing budget should include a large portion dedicated to getting the NEW customer in the door. The person who isn't aware you exist. The customer who is unfamiliar with your area. Since bringing repeat customers *back* in the door is on the shoulders of operations and not marketing, stop putting all of your eggs in the social media/database growing/loyalty app department. No matter how good your marketing approach is, if the customer didn't have an awesome experience the first time, no amount of marketing dollars will bring them back. Focus your budget instead on where the undecided customers already are—Google, Yelp, and TripAdvisor. Optimize your profiles and respond to all of your reviews. These big three are the customer's first impression of your brand. *They are the catalysts.* If you fail step one of customer acquisition, nothing else really matters. You'll never be able to measure the number of people who never walk in your door.

Make your presentation amazing and Instagrammable. Ask yourself if your customer's experience creates a reason for them to bring it up around friends or co-workers. What do you offer that is "buzz-worthy" in today's world of viral videos and three-second attention spans? We aren't just making burgers anymore. We're creating memories. As cheesy as that sounds, it's true now more than ever before. Remember that nothing brings more people in the door than word of mouth. No amount of marketing will *ever* top this. Word of mouth can be your best friend or your worst enemy, so make sure that the memories created are great ones.

Employ the best personalities out there and pay accordingly. Nothing raises morale like being appreciated. Being a great boss is a necessary building block to a happy staff, but if they can't make their bills with the money they're making, they will eventually move on to greener pastures.

Nothing in this business is guaranteed, with the possible exception of things getting tougher and tougher as we evolve. Competition is fierce and will most definitely get more intense as the years go on. This is the hardest job that you could possibly tackle that requires zero formal education. Just like the odds of a celebrity marriage lasting, chances are you will fail at this. With a ton of planning, some great people, and a shitload of luck, you may also be one of the successful ones. Good luck out there!

–Erik

LET'S WORK TOGETHER!

I'd love to help you with your Google presence. Let's start putting your brand in front of every potential new customer possible! Not every bar or restaurant needs help however, but how do we know where you rank currently? I will scan your business and send you a snapshot of where you rank in the Google results and where your competition ranks as well. A typical scan looks like this:

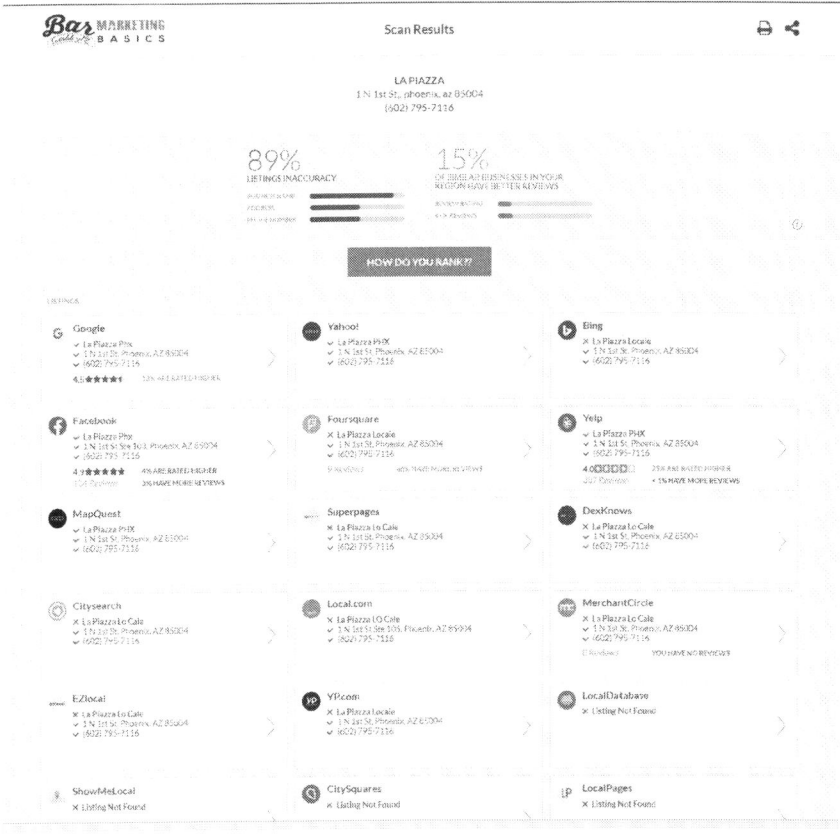

If you notice, errors can be simply missing info or your brand can be missing from a directory altogether. It could also mean something as simple as an inconsistent name. In this case, humans know that "La Piazza Phx" is the same place as "La Piazza Locale" but Google tends to get confused by these subtle differences. If Google's confidence in your info drops, so does your Google ranking. If your business is in the 89% inaccurate range like this example, SEO will produce a considerable amount of positive change. Most businesses are around the percentage of this example however. It's no one's fault, it's just where most businesses will default to if SEO is not taken into consideration. If your business has around 20% inaccuracies or lower, chances are you already have your SEO situation handled and additional work won't make a ton of progress. Once these issues are addressed, Google takes notice and your ranking will absolutely rise over the course of months and even years into the future.

Request your own report at https://barmarketingbasics.com and I'll be happy to scan your business and send you the free report.

A SELFISH REQUEST

Just like your online review volume and rating with Google, Amazon expands my book's reach to more people based on how many reviews I receive on my Amazon page. So PLEASE leave me an honest review if I've provided any value for you. If this book was a total waste of time, let me know that as well! The more reviews the book gets, the more new people will see my book as an option. The essence of self-perpetuation. I really, really appreciate you making it all the way through this. Thank you so much. You are a 5-star person in my book!

–Erik Shellenberger

ABOUT THE AUTHOR

Erik Shellenberger has been in the restaurant and bar industry since he was thirteen years old and worked for his mother in the food and beverage department at a Utah ski resort. Since then, he has held every position from dishwasher to bartender to marketing director and everything in between. With a decade of corporate marketing experience, he has gone from student to teacher and now runs Bar Marketing Basics (barmarketingbasics.com). He has quickly grown his client base, expanding beyond his hometown of Scottsdale, Arizona, into Los Angeles CA and has connected with clients across the nation, as far away as the East Coast.

Made in the
USA
Middletown, DE